D0233944

Say One For Me

Also by Wesley Carr and published by SPCK:

*Brief Encounters: Pastoral Ministry through the
Occasional Offices* (1985)

*The Pastor as Theologian: The Integration of Pastoral Ministry,
Theology and Discipleship* (1989)

Ministry and the Media (1990)

Manifold Wisdom: Christians in the New Age (1991)

Say One For Me

THE CHURCH OF ENGLAND IN THE NEXT DECADE

Wesley Carr

with

Paul Bates   David Conner   John Cox
Graham James   Christopher Lewis   Bernice Martin
Stephen Platten   Robert Reiss   Timothy Stevens
Angela Tilby

First published in Great Britain 1992
SPCK
Marylebone Road
London NW1 4DU

© Wesley Carr 1992

All rights reserved. No part of this book may be reproduced
or transmitted in any form or by any means, electronic or
mechanical, including photocopying, recording, or by any
information storage and retrieval system, without permission
in writing from the publisher.

British Library Cataloguing-in-Publication Data

A Catalogue record for this book is available from the British Library

Typeset by Pioneer Associates, Perthshire
Printed in Great Britain by
The Longdunn Press Ltd, Bristol

'Say one for me'

— a remark often made to clergy
and to lay people on their way to church

CONTENTS

Contents

INTRODUCTION

Every book needs to be written with a specific reader in mind. Ours has been the new Archbishop of Canterbury. This is not grandiosity on our part. We began meeting as a group about the time when the selection of the next Archbishop of Canterbury was beginning to be discussed. We therefore focused our thinking by asking ourselves, What will be specifically expected of an archbishop in the next decade and what sort of church will he anticipate leading? George Carey's appointment was announced, earlier than we had foreseen, as we were concluding our work. We completed this book before his enthronement.

The appointment of a new archbishop, however, is routine compared with the change which the Church of England is facing. This often seems mystifying. In particular it is unclear to what extent it is self-inflicted or a response to transformations in the world of which the church is part. We believe that this sense of change is a sign of the church's continued vitality within English society. The experience of incomprehensible change is common to many institutions in Europe, both East and West. The problem is certainly not peculiar to the Church of England; it is more widespread, complex and profound than it sometimes appears in synods and other church debates. In the church it is usually simplified into a discussion about the personality and competence of church leaders, especially the bishops and archbishops. But the issue is more serious than this: it is about institutional survival. It is, therefore, as the leader of an institution, not as a particular individual, that we have held the archbishop in mind.

At first sight survival might not seem to be a proper concern. Christians aspire to be able, if required, to lose their lives in the service of the gospel. But that personal surrender which may be the mark of individual discipleship is not an option for an institutional church, especially one like the Church of England which is assigned by people other than its members a range of functions – some hardly discerned within the church itself.

1

Christians believe that God has a future: that hope is part of their creed. But about the futures of churches there must always be less conviction. Nevertheless, most Christians would still confess to some faith in the church, even if specific churches may apostatize and go out of existence through decay or ecumenical amalgamation. But even with this conviction we remain uncomfortably aware from history that under God churches can and do (and on reflection we might say sometimes deserve to) disappear. The fate of the powerful and privileged church of North Africa is one of the most notable examples. So survival is in fact an issue for churches, especially one like the Church of England with its inheritance of privilege within one nation.

This is a book written from the perspective of optimistic, but realistic, conviction. We believe that there is a continuing, specific and, we dare also say, God-given vocation for the Church of England which is expressed in terms of its ministry to and with people and in a distinctive theological argument for its existence. Yet both are under threat: there is a pressure for withdrawal into a sectarian mentality, under the specious guise of 'wholeness' and 'full' commitment to the gospel, coupled with theological uncertainty about whether the continuance of this particular church can be justified. In local ecumenical projects the Anglicans are usually the least ecclesiologically sophisticated, often to the dismay of their fellow Christians.

Graham James and Wesley Carr convened the group. We first met because, from our different perspectives, we were concerned about and loyal to our church. The positions which we at present hold, and our recent experience, have brought us into working contact with many aspects of the life of the Church of England – dioceses, parishes, bishops, clergy, laity, synods and councils. We each also have links with other groups in our society and beyond. Several of us were friends before the group assembled; and all of us now would count each other as such. Most of us already respected one another's different perspectives on theology, the church and ministry. But we were, and are, primarily united by a conviction that what we are discussing matters to many more people than just ourselves. Our debates and the discipline of writing have clarified our thinking and, we like to believe, minimized our reliance on personal prejudice. The result is, we

2

trust, theologically literate but practically oriented, since we have tried to write out of our knowledge and experience. It is an invitation to fellow members of the Church of England to take these ideas further.

A further clarification is needed in this ecumenical age. Can we justify a preoccupation with the Church of England? At one level the answer is simple: it is our church, the one we know best and the one for which we have some responsibility in our different roles. But there is a more serious reason for our stance. Whatever the original aspirations of the ecumenical movement, it is becoming clear that the distinctiveness of different churches – their polity, theological emphases, styles of worship and tasks – is a continuing and significant factor in the total witness of the Church of God. To draw attention to distinctiveness is not to be in any sense anti-ecumenical. Indeed, it increasingly seems probable that the liveliness of the various churches is mutually interdependent. The Free Churches, for example, may need a vigorous Church of England from which to dissent and so energize their own characteristic vocation. Seen in this light our concern with our own church will contribute to the possibility of genuinely ecumenical endeavour and, more importantly, achievement.

The constitution of the Church of England, therefore, needs attention. This is especially necessary as the churches together enter the Decade of Evangelism. There is already evidence of a variety of approaches to this subject. One clarification of evangelism, for example, could be through mutual recognition of the different responsibilities which the various churches possess. In these chapters we indicate where we believe that of the contemporary Church of England lies. We hope, therefore, that our argument will interest and stimulate members of other churches as much as those who lead our own.

The end of a century is not a time for pretentious visions and we certainly do not assuredly regard ourselves as seers. Too much has happened in this century for anyone casually to express confidence in the long-term. The danger, however, in such circumstances is that we nonchalantly abandon the past in the hope of short-term gain, which is 'authenticated' by being treated as a sign of the new world. By contrast we have tried to offer an argument for another period (Who knows how long?) of useful activity by the Church of England. By 'useful' we mean useful both to God and to those among whom he has set us. Such a programme may, if read superficially, appear conservative and even curmudgeonly. We hope that none of us has yet declined to that state. We argue that the Church of England is changing and, what is more important, achieves more transformation in the lives of individuals, groups and society than is often realized and that there is no reason why that process should now cease.

At this point introductions usually offer thanks and disclaimers. We cannot disclaim, because it is our book. We each severally and together own it and offer it. The thanks for ideas and insights are too many to mention. Our policy on notes demonstrates this. We have kept them to a strict minimum, only acknowledging quotations. We are all privileged to have known, and know, able and interesting people. We do, however, especially thank Julie James and Rosslie Platten for welcoming us into their homes and offering generous and soothing hospitality, tinged with some astringent realism, after each session of debate.

The Authors
March 1991

THE AUTHORS

The book has been written by Wesley Carr from the discussions of the group and the individual contributions of each member. These are acknowledged at the head of each chapter and source critics might have some fun with stylistic incongruities. All have worked through the whole and, in that sense, this is a collaborative effort which we all own.

Paul Bates	Canon of Westminster
Wesley Carr	Dean of Bristol
David Conner	Vicar of Great St Mary's, Cambridge
John Cox	Vicar of the Ecumenical Parish of Roehampton
Graham James	Chaplain to the Archbishop of Canterbury
Christopher Lewis	Canon Residentiary of Canterbury
Bernice Martin	Emeritus Reader in Sociology, University of London
Stephen Platten	The Archbishop of Canterbury's Secretary for Ecumenical Affairs
Robert Reiss	Team Rector of Grantham
Timothy Stevens	Archdeacon of West Ham
Angela Tilby	Producer of Religious Programmes, BBC Television

1

IS THERE A FUTURE FOR THE CHURCH OF ENGLAND?

The opening chapter discusses whether the Church of England has, or even deserves, a future. It possesses certain characteristics which are historically determined and which, although they have changed in form over the years, nevertheless remain significant. What has changed is the amount of agreement about how they are to be evaluated. In practical terms they point to the continuance of an interpretative ministry (perhaps a modern way of describing a 'learned ministry') and a parochially ordered structure. The ideas in this chapter are largely contributed by Wesley Carr.

Whether there remains a distinctive role for the Church of England in the last decade of the twentieth century is the central question addressed in this book. From time to time it is voiced both inside and outside the church. It can appear morbidly introverted, as when church members speculate about the way in which the church is changing and wonder whether their energies are being well spent. More often it is linked to a larger and less defined sense of historical inevitability. Because the Church of England is, the argument goes, so deeply embedded in an English culture which is itself in process of profound change, its survival is in question. And an era in which statistics are provided for every facet of human life draws attention to the obvious decline in public religious behaviour, which has been in England customarily expressed through the Church of England.

The question of the Church of England's survival is usually posed in the context of one or more of the following issues.

Divisions

Divisions in the Church of England, which have hitherto been mainly contained, are now becoming so critical that a consensus can no longer be sustained. The old familiar splits persist, such as those discerned between Catholic and Reformed (Evangelical). The two wings, however, also seem to unite in the face of another grouping – 'the liberal establishment'. But things are not so simple and complicated relationships and even conspiracies are descried. The public politicizing of the church through the synodical system has replaced more discreet ways of acknowledging differences. If the divergences were felt only at one level, say that of the General Synod, we might discount them. But there is a feeling that at the heart of the church's parishes, too, they are re-emerging with greater force and might not be manageable much longer. For the present they usually focus around the issue of the ordination of women, but that is probably a symptom rather than a cause.

It is frequently forgotten that the Church of England has never been united in any obvious sense. Its life, because it is concerned with things that ultimately matter – God, as well as the nature of society – is generated through conflict, which may itself be one of the marks of any lively church. The complexity and comprehensiveness of the Church of England, however, means that it seems to possess a unique facility for converting legitimate competition which occurs between churches, though it is rarely acknowledged, into a damaging intra-church struggle. There is, therefore, a perennial question about how much conflict should be borne and how much it can be sustained without the membership of the institution declining into a debilitated quarrelsome few.

Establishment

This is an enduring issue, both within and outside the church. Some ask whether the establishment has ever been justifiable; more today wonder whether there remains any reason for it. Relations with the Crown and government constantly need to be scrutinized. But we also need to be careful about what we mean (and what others mean) by 'establishment'.

Any society (however plural it may become) seems to possess (or, if lacking, to seek) a sense of an order which undergirds the confusions of everyday life. This may be symbolized by 'establishment'. The 'order' does not necessarily come from a common belief which commands widespread assent. But it is sustained through the commitment of some to a vision which they are allowed (and indeed we might say requested) to hold for others. Where, for example, we might ask, has the church ever not been in some sense part of an establishment?

One useful clarification of this complex notion is to draw a distinction between 'high' and 'earthed' establishment. High establishment is represented by the legal and historical inter-twining of the church with the nation. It is symbolized by the presence of bishops in the House of Lords, the status of the Archbishop of Canterbury and the continuance of parliamentary concern with ecclesiastical legislation. There is also, however, the 'earthed' establishment, by which the Church of England orders itself parochially so that it has someone – a parson or *persona* – to whom is assigned responsibility first for a parish and only secondly for a congregation. This is an acknowledgement of an assumption about the nature of the church, as a body with frayed edges, which encourages association as a means to ministry rather than membership as a means to belief.

Although the percentages vary considerably according to social setting, the Church of England still baptizes approximately a third of babies and performs about a third of all marriages, and many funerals. Why do many of those who profess no allegiance and make no pretence at membership or belief, act as though the Church of England belongs to them? For example, the closure of a church – even an undistinguished building and one where there is no longer a congregation – usually creates an outcry. When the Alternative Service Book was introduced in 1980, avowed agnostics and professing atheists publicly abused the Church of England for removing what they claimed belonged to them.

Both facets of establishment are controversial. But whenever the argument re-emerges, we need to recognize that the idea of an 'established' church is not merely an Erastian error: it is a specific ecclesiology not necessarily of privilege but potentially of duty and ministry. The 'high' without the 'earthed' is no establishment at all, but the 'earthed' needs its corresponding acknowledgement at other levels of a society.

Ecumenism

The leaders of the Church of England played a major role in creating the World Council of Churches and in spite of many reservations, this church still takes its place in that organization. Local ecumenism is also in general supported, and often led, by the Church of England, even if the General Synod has been nervous of Anglo–Methodist relations or the Covenant. This ecumenical age generates two messages: on the one hand there is a sense that the longed-for 'new' church could now come about. On the other hand, such relations require of the participants a greater self-definition than may hitherto have been achieved or required. A loosely structured church is likely to be caught between these two ideals, neither of which it can attain. The Church of England is not particularly strong on the rationale for distinctive ecclesiologies, and especially one for itself. It has taken a more pragmatic approach, which pays off in terms of the practice of ministry but may encourage self-doubt in inter-church relations.

Organization

One consequence of this pragmatism has been that the Church of England appears at first sight to have been largely unorganized for much of its existence. In fact, there is a subtle and not easily accessible design to the way that the church works. The basic thrust of its organization has been to be able to engage with people, whatever the form of society. Certain fundamentals have made this possible, among them the clinging to the notion of a wider church – the church catholic – by retaining episcopal government and to being available by maintaining the idea and ideal of the parochial system. Its organization tends to develop in an accumulative fashion, usually adding bits and not deliberately removing others until they decay. The nature of patronage and

9

the incumbent's freehold provide interesting instances. Over the years the way in which they have been perceived and used has changed, sometimes by legal enactment but more often by assumption. The continued attention which is given to them should direct a pragmatic church's thoughts to what it is actually about rather than to theories of ministry and order.

This century (especially the years since the Second World War) has seen a further bureaucratizing of the church, with a consequent diminishing of efforts to justify its activity theologically. There is, for instance, a major problem as to whether this sort of church can sustain – or should attempt to sustain – a synodical form of government and whether this is appropriate to an episcopally ordered church which has a specific task of offering its ministry to parishioners in general rather than church members. Undoubtedly the relations between General, diocesan and deanery synods (not to mention Parochial Church Councils) are not yet right, either in the way each functions within the system or in the balance of power between them. And if, as seems to be a contemporary thrust (for instance, in the recent review of the infrastructure of the General Synod), the synodical system diminishes, or even attempts to remove, the influence of the episcopate, then what sort of church is left?

Context

These familiar questions seem to arise chiefly from within the Church. For the Church of England, however, as for all churches, there is now a new and more daunting issue: what place, if any, does (and will) religion occupy in a pluralist society? And even if religion is increasingly regarded as a private matter, what is the standing and function of religious institutions – churches? Assumptions about secular pluralism, its nature and impact, need to be scrutinized, especially when they are invoked by church people. But even if it can be argued that religion as a general phenomenon retains some place in the life of our society, this does not free us from the key question for the church: namely, can a particular religion, in this instance Christianity, retain a distinctive place and, what is more, can a specific form of that religion (the Church of England) continue to claim a unique status?

But if these are some of the areas of doubt, we can by contrast discern three contemporary emphases which are adduced as grounds for confidence about the continuance of the Church of England. Each relates to some of the historical processes which have created this Church.

Liturgy

It has often been argued that the Church of England coheres around a common liturgy rather than some specific doctrine or ministerial order. Whatever else may happen, so the argument goes, the church's diversity is held together by the Book of Common Prayer. When the Alternative Service Book was introduced, it was emphasized that this was not to displace the old but a complementary alternative to (and therefore congruent with) the old in function. The emptiness of this argument, however, is, and has been, evident at least since the controversies over the revision of the Prayer Book in 1928, and probably even earlier with the legal battles over ritualism in the nineteenth century.

Why, then, is the contention still made? The answer may be that, because there are so few undisputed points of coherence, one that is defensible in theory but need not be tested in practice is most convenient. For aberrant liturgical practices can always be justified in terms of missionary zeal or local need. Thus, while they may not seem to be connected with the holding function of the Prayer Book, they can be rationalized as within the spirit of common prayer – a typically Anglican argument.

The 'via media'

If there is any single theological stance that has been historically claimed to be that of the Church of England, it is probably that of the *via media*. The technical sense in which this phrase was originally used has largely been discounted. In popular thought it has been equated with moderation, which in turn leads to the elevation of tolerance as a virtue. It is, however, a powerful concept of a theological method which is worthy of defence. From Jewel, Hooker and Andrewes to Maurice, Gore, Temple and Ramsey, a method has been created which gives priority to God and the unknowability of faith rather than to merely agreement to differ. In 1990, announcing the creation of the Michael Ramsey Chair in Theology at the University of Kent, Robert Runcie characterized Ramsey as a man of 'thoughtful holiness', which well describes the quintessence of Anglican theology and practice. At its best it is marked by these two characteristics. First there is thoughtfulness, a gently sceptical attitude towards the certainties which other Christians may display. The second mark is holiness, a sense that in the end all that matters is a sense of the presence of God, which is usually found in public worship and the spirituality of prayers learned and repeated by rote.

The Pastoral Basis

If, however, today the Church of England has abandoned the idea of common prayer and lost some confidence in the *via media*, there is less doubt about a third basic stance: the pastoral basis of its activity. Anglican clergy have customarily been a little vain about their 'pastoral' attitude. While being willing to acknowledge incompetence at preaching and even being proud of ineffectiveness in administration, they have retained a sense of themselves as pre-eminently pastors. But the notion of 'pastoral' extends beyond that of care for individuals. Included in it has been the idea of service to the nation as a whole, or to all people, without regard to their personal belief, or to the parish, the local community. The vicar is still appointed to 'the cure of souls', which means more than merely 'care'. It implies having before God responsibility for their destiny, an ideal which is articulated in the ordinal of the Book of Common Prayer and which continues to inspire the finest parish priests. One prominent dimension to this pastoring has been the pastor's willingness to engage with and respond to what is, now significantly with increasing disparagement, called 'folk religion'.

The Created Church

Any inquiry about the Church of England must begin by asking, 'existence of what?'. There is an institutional reality to the Church of England, which is best conceived as consisting of a range of interactions between people. There is, for instance, whatever happens between a vicar and the people he meets. The connection is not limited to what occurs in a personal meeting: he represents something about 'the church', which those who engage with him also have in their minds. Their interaction, what goes on between them, contributes to the creation of the church. The same is true of the daily activity of lay Christians. Some of these interactions are easy to discern: they consist of actual meetings. Some are more tentative, such as, for instance, the relationship between a community and its church building and what it expects to happen there. Generally, however, this link will be articulated only when it is felt to be going awry. For the rest of the time it is covert but nonetheless felt.

Any human institution is constructed like this. But it is especially important when considering a church that we acknowledge the significance of its interactive nature. For when we think carefully about what a church does, it is both very simple and rather strange. Church members are volunteers. Whatever their motivation to believe, in human terms there is no compulsion. On the basis of their faith these volunteers offer to serve other people, whether as individuals, groups or at a deeper level in some sense 'society'. Those so served are, however, usually unaware of (and, as evangelists often discover, uninterested in) the motivation of the servers and take such activity for granted. They expect, for instance, the church building to be kept up but they are aghast at the thought that they might pay – except when disaster looms, when they will usually still support an appeal.

Not surprisingly frustration sometimes breaks out. This is not confined to the clergy. For example, a congregation may complain about the presence of people who bring their babies for baptism during the main Sunday service. These 'strangers' are disrupting 'our' life. But such stresses are not distractions: they point to the core of the nature of the institution. In a church of this sort the quality of interaction between different parts mirrors or illuminates that at other points. So, for instance, what goes on between worshippers is not something that happens privately. It also contains – although it is not always obvious – aspects of other connections and interchanges, such as those between the church as a whole and the community in which it is set or between God and his world.

For instance, when a mother comes to worship with her child, she is not just Janet or Mary: she can regard herself, and be held by others in the congregation, as representing something of another group to which she belongs – the mothers of the area – before God. If they can grasp this, those trying to run a church can free themselves from some constricting limitations. It is a significant perception, for example, for any creative thinking about mission and ministry or prophecy and pastoring, or any other of the polarities which loom large in most church discussions.

When examined from this perspective, clearly no church generates itself in some private social or spiritual context. Debates about ecclesiastical origins and tradition and their legitimacy, whilst important and necessary, are insufficient to account for the existence of a particular church. Churches function within contexts, even when they delude themselves into thinking that somehow they are separate from the demands of their environment. Even those who reject the world need the world in order to be able to base their life on that rejection.

One strength of the Church of England's perception of itself has been the high profile that it gives to this interactive and creative sense of 'church'. Indeed it seems here, rather than in any of the usually proposed alternatives, that the distinctiveness of the Church of England can be discerned. A common liturgy, mutual toleration or an emphasis on pastoral ministry are all crucial points of continuing public interaction. But they do not themselves sustain it.

The need for clarity at this point is the key to all that follows in this book. Amid the tensions and arguments about the nature of the church and what it should be doing, such perspicacity will enable its ministers to think and become organizationally, pastorally and liturgically more competent.

By contrast confusion here leads to the weakness in much

current thinking about the church. For example, thinking about pastoral reorganization may need to become more alert to this dynamic basis of the church rather than to its geographical, or even less its numerical, design. The government of such an institution is likely to depend more on 'feel' than organizational niceties, which is why the style of bishops and other leaders remains persistently important in the working of the dioceses and parishes.

Aim and Task

One helpful way of thinking about such a loosely structured institution as a church is to draw a distinction between 'aims' and 'task'. Obviously the words are virtually synonymous. But for clarity in this context we might suggest that, for example, the *aim* of a liturgy is to ensure that the worship of God is done worthily – a very suitable intention for a church. But that does not account for the significance of worship for the continued existence, or even survival, of that church. This depends on the *task* which a church has to perform, which is what it must keep doing in order to continue. Such a task might be less accessible than worship but no less important. For example, we may suggest that the Church of England distinctively has the *task* of affirming the continuing importance of that dimension to human life which is felt to be irrational, that is, which all find difficulty in acknowledging but which emerges from time to time unexpectedly in people's lives. This connects in one way with worship; after all, what is logically more irrational than worship? But it puts that distinctive activity in the larger context of human experience, where the irrational, that which cannot easily be categorized, has somehow to be acknowledged, if it is not to be too frightening to be borne.

For institutional clarity we need continually to be alert to the question of task and not confuse it with aims. Similarly our theological formulations about the church need to be congruent with this organizational device.

Such phenomena are not merely a matter of academic interest. They take us to the core of the nature of the Church of England: it is still assumed by many to be available to them and it is trusted to remain so. Recent controversies within the Church of England seem largely to derive from the church's current inability to perceive this basis of its interactive existence. The contribution of the external context is decreasingly acknowledged in the internal workings of the church. The result is a developing uncertainty about what the Church of England is and especially where it is to seek to base the search for its identity.

It is not enough, however, merely to assert, and even affirm, the contrary position. We have to ask whether this range of activity constitutes a legitimate role for a Christian church and, if it does, how it should be exercised. Ecclesiologies tend to be constructed in response to experienced change. It would be foolish and presumptuous to suggest that the Church of England presents a paradigm of the fulness of divine action. It does, however, represent a significant dimension – the involvement of the divine in every aspect of life and a God who is willing always to lose rather than save himself and to risk being misunderstood by others.

The behaviour of the Church of England in this respect correlates with one of its chief areas of academic distinction: some of the best Anglican thinking has been in the theology of the incarnation. Perhaps of all the primary Christian doctrines this one touches the area in which the Church of England, both academically and pastorally, operates instinctively and where its existence is negotiated, whether locally (as in the parishes) or on a wider front.

An Interpretative Ministry

Such activity demands an interpretative style of ministry. The task of the Church of England, often but not always performed through its clergy, may be described as to interpret people's experiences of life in relation to God, thus putting them into a divine perspective. This is one reason why liturgy has been so central to Anglican practice. It is not in fact the text of the Book of Common Prayer or the Alternative Service Book that holds the disparate parts of the Church of England together, but a common approach, whatever the superficial differences, to the centrality and importance of worship for its own sake. In worship the experiences of worshippers (and they need not necessarily be distinctively Christian) are less transformed than re-contextualized.

16

In its new perspective people discover hitherto hidden dimensions and wonders in their lives.

A Parochial Framework

If the style of the Church of England's ministry is interpretative, the framework which makes this possible is parochial. Parishes are best conceived as human groupings defined by geographical reference. The two go hand in hand, so that the interlocking and demanding facets of human life with which the church's ministers deal are discovered to be limited and sufficiently manageable for anyone to risk engaging in such activity. The distinctiveness of the parish concept is worth valuing, because it locates the church's ministry by reference to the complexities of people's lives and not by the presumed nature of the congregation. Whatever the different details of each parish, this overarching concept defines the church's ministerial stance and is of continuing importance.

Conclusion

The Church of England has a determinable vocation which is always to be discovered through interaction with its context. This engagement and its significance for all concerned is easily lost through carelessness. But responsible Anglicans will not quickly surrender it. For without it we may argue that there is a loss to people in general in our society (and not just the believers), to the Church universal and to theological endeavour. We need to fight for this stance, without overlooking its limitations.

The points outlined in this opening chapter are all examined more fully on the following pages. We first consider four very familiar Anglican topics: parish ministry, worship and liturgy, ordination and the relation between the 'centre' and the rest of the church. We then move to a wider field of debate: a modern alternative to the traditional parish which is created by the media, the notion of common ground, as preserved in cathedrals, and the problems of a synodically ordered episcopal church. And finally we consider this church in its cultural setting and what it may represent there, concluding with an outline of the sort of theological thinking that might both undergird and provide a critique for the stance proposed in our argument.

2

PARISH EXPECTATIONS

Traditionally the strength of the Church of England has been seen to lie in its work with people on the ground in the parishes. In spite of various arguments which have been proposed against this structure, it has proved to be surprisingly resilient. The argument of the chapter is based upon the experiences of two parish priests, Bob Reiss and David Conner. There remain greater expectations of the 'vicar' than he or she sometimes realizes. These persist, even if expressed in different ways from hitherto.

English travellers arriving in Istanbul can have no doubt that they are in a Muslim country. The skyline is dominated by mosques and the initial impact is powerfully 'foreign'. They know immediately that they are away from home. Familiarity with the English countryside may blind those same people to the equally prominent cultural role of church buildings in this country. In most villages and towns the tower or spire of the parish church is one of the most easily recognizable symbols of that place. These buildings almost define Englishness and for many they contribute to the vague, but comforting, sense of 'being at home'. The church is expected to be there, even if usually noticed only when it is not. Any attempt to demolish it, or even sometimes alter its appearance, is usually resisted strongly, not least by those who may rarely, if ever, worship there. Church buildings have a representative function, both symbolizing the place and enshrining (and maybe awakening) the religious aspirations of a community.

Expectations of the Clergy

But what of the clergy associated with those churches? People seem to expect there to be a vicar at the church. But for what do

18

they look to him? The answers vary and are often contradictory. But they have one thing in common: they are serious and they make demands on the parish priest's attention and time.

There are, for example, expectations of his family. People look for a good son, husband or parent and sometimes treat members of the vicar's family as if they were their property. This is compounded by the way that his job comes into the heart of the home to an extent, and more importantly in an unmanageable fashion, that is unusual for most other professions. His office may be in the family house, which is in any case only loaned to him. It is not property with which the members of his family may do with as they wish. People who want to contact the vicar are likely to do so at times when his family might reasonably expect to see something of him – meal times, evenings and weekends: 'I'm sorry to call at lunch-time, vicar, but I know how busy you are and knew you would be here.' A priest who is sensitive to his family's needs will feel uncomfortably caught between their expectations and the requirements of his public role.

A second level of expectation derives from members of the congregation. They naturally look to him to order the worship, to preach intelligible and preferably interesting sermons, and to be in contact with organizations sponsored by the church. Individuals also treat him as their personal chaplain: he should visit them regularly (more often than is practicable), be available to counsel them in their sadness, share with them in their joy, act as friend to their family and be a personal spiritual guide. Although it sounds, and, if done properly, is demanding, this work is not inevitably a burden. It is the core of the parish priest's ministry. With average luck he should find kindred spirits with whom friendship and exploration of matters of faith and life is a pleasure. Ministry then becomes a privilege. But in other cases the demands may tax his tolerance, particularly when he realizes that when he fails to meet them cruel criticism will swiftly follow.

Beyond the boundaries of the congregation and family, however, lies the most intractable area, which is often called, and sometimes dismissed as, 'the fringe'. This is composed of people who will from time to time make contact with the church, assuming it to be 'theirs' and that they are 'members'. Obvious instances of such connection are the occasional offices of baptism,

19

marriage and burial or the major festivals. But some also feel attached through being friends with someone who is already linked to the church and through whom they believe they have direct access to 'their' vicar.

This investment of hope is not misplaced. The sick, elderly, housebound and disadvantaged, for example, are instinctively recognized by almost all clergy as the traditional recipients of such pastoral care. When people appear who seem less deserving of attention, however, they are dismissed as 'the fringe'. Any work with such people may not obviously lead to enlarged congregations. Most members of the church may recognize the legitimacy of such ministry by their vicar. But there always seem to be some who will not. Seeking to build up the congregation and thus achieving some measure of growth is the route to ecclesiastical popularity in a culture which places a premium on visible success. But while some clergy may work with that end in mind, others will be unhappy at any suggestion that Christian ministry is offered in the hope of some return. They see these implicit requests as human longings to which they should respond out of Christian love. This sort of ministry is, therefore, valid in itself, a proper response to human religious need.

The wishes of individuals may seem limitless. But on top of these there are the expectations of institutions within the parish. Some of these have a long-standing tradition of chaplaincy – for example, hospitals, barracks, industry and commerce. Others look for clergy support – schools wanting a prominent local figure for their governing body, or the management committees of voluntary social work organizations. The vicar's involvement in such activity is normally accepted by congregations as legitimate. Beyond such institutions, however, there are in most parishes other secular bodies where, if contact is to be made with the church, it will come only if the clergy take the initiative. Places of work, where there has been no industrial chaplaincy, sports clubs, and local government offices are all spots where the vicar is generally still welcome as a guest, providing he does not ostentatiously proselytize or moralize. There may be few expectations on the part of the institutions themselves that he will make contact. But some clergy still feel that something should be attempted in their parish and so initiate this sort of connection.

Those who attempt such a ministry are constantly surprised by the warmth of the welcome. Bishops find that they only have to hint that they might be interested in a visit and the formal invitation is made almost instantaneously. The Bishop of Stepney, for example, wrote about his work in the East End of London; the job, he said, is like being a permanent mayor: 'Plunging into schools, businesses and community groups, being asked everywhere. Bishops have their uses because they encounter the whole of society.'[1]

Parochial clergy can offer similar instances. But we should be careful: this welcome is not universal. A vicar in London approached the offices of part of the BBC which happened to be located in his parish. He was met with uncomprehending astonishment that he should visit at all. The mind-set of the people was national: they did not see themselves as local in any sense. By contrast the priest saw them as part of 'his' locality – the parish. Such a ministry requires, therefore, some congruence between the focus of activity of the institution concerned and that of the church which the minister represents.

Sometimes the local vicar is the right person for this engagement; at another level of entry into the community it may be the bishop; and sometimes it may be a person, such as a chaplain, whose remit may transcend parochial and even diocesan boundaries. It is frequently easier, for example, for the incumbent of a town-centre church to gain access to organizations which serve that town as a whole than for the vicar of the suburban parish in which they are technically set. But once the contact by anyone from the church has been established, while hesitations may remain relating either to the fear of proselytizing or of the church taking sides in the institution's internal politics, the welcome is usually generous and open. Indeed, if the vicar or chaplain subsequently breaks the relationship in an apparently casual fashion, disproportionate anger ensues.

The Reasons for such Expectations

By why? Why do people in these institutions still today welcome the church's involvement in some form or other? Four reasons may be suggested.

21

First, in places like hospitals, factories or barracks, those responsible for initiating and maintaining the invitation talk about the chaplain's care for individuals. In each case he or she is usually expected to be introduced to newcomers and may be called in at a time of personal crisis, such as a suicide attempt, injury, the death of relatives or, with increasing frequency, redundancy. The institution appears to welcome the presence of someone who is in the system but not part of it, who represents concern for individuals in their own right, and who can offer such care without having any personal status to uphold. Some industrial chaplains, for example, seem to be able to do something for the man or woman made redundant that is beyond the capacity of personnel officers, however caring they might be.

Secondly, the fact that chaplains are organizationally outside the power structures gives them a freedom that the institution values. The Army, for example, articulately a secular organization, respects the chaplain's role. When the newspapers were full of allegations of bullying and brutality in the Army, one senior officer said that he and other senior officers thought that the chaplain's presence and independence, as well as the Army's respect for the chaplain's confidentiality and his right of direct access to the Commanding Officer, gave him a significant role in dealing with something about which all were extremely concerned but uncertain how to respond. They acknowledged the need for ministry.

Thirdly, some secular bodies value the presence of representatives of the wider community in their organization. School governors or voluntary social work organizations wish to be accountable to the wider community. Often they simply want someone 'out there' to know what is going on. Clergy are, they hope, available as members of that wider community. Because of the way in which they are invited to move through various levels of the community, they are assumed to have useful knowledge and an overview which may be denied to others. Institutions are not, of course, averse to trying to harness such political power as the church might be believed to wield. So, coupled with the institution's wish to have representatives of the wider community, there often goes a further wish to find allies. Other organizations may value such a presence for different reasons. The involvement of a vicar or bishop may be thought to give them legitimacy, particularly in the case of a new development that may be questioned or even resented in the community. When clergy respond to such requests they have the chance of offering at least an informed critique, provided that they are doing their basic work of moving through and ministering in the wider community and do not rely on the specious ground of special revelation because they are Christian.

Fourthly, behind all these factors there is something, which is not often clearly articulated, about the clergy and the church having to do with God. At a time of bewildering change, a body which is believed to stand for stability and permanence, a still point in a turning world, is esteemed for this reason alone. The church, especially through its representatives – the clergy – is held to stand for values that transcend the immediate aims of the welcoming institution. Because of this the church has a distinctive relationship to some institutions, which can scarcely be acknowledged but which seems from time to time to be deeply felt. By praying, for example, for people in times of stress, ministers are believed to be in touch with unmanageable forces within which the whole world has to function. The presence of clergy allows people to acknowledge their ultimate dependence, which is always felt rather than understood. The evidence is, therefore, that the clergy are expected to talk confidently about God and ultimate meaning without becoming too transparently religious or too closely identified with those among whom they move.

An interesting illustration of the delicacy of this area arises around the Non-Stipendiary Ministry. This began as a supplementary ministry to that of the full-time clergy – Auxiliary Pastoral Ministry – although it rapidly took on a life of its own and changed its name. It was an experiment which has never been formally evaluated, in spite of numerous reports and discussions. One key idea was that ordained ministers might pioneer a presence in their place of work. Some now use the term 'Ministers in Secular Employment' (MSE) to describe these ministers. Their implied function has shifted from assisting to spearheading the church's activity within the world of work in a different, though not wholly clear, fashion from that of chaplains.

In the light of these intentions it is, therefore, intriguing to note that the British armed forces will not allow serving personnel to become non-stipendiary ministers. The services, in which the clergyman's role is still valued, believe that it is not possible to combine what they expect of the ordained minister with other roles with which it may conflict. They appear to regard it as important to preserve a distinctive role for the priest. At this point the church's wishes and those of a group to whom ministry is offered, conflict. A similar message came from industry when John Tiller was researching in 1982. It was reported that, when asked for comment, leaders in industry and the trades unions valued the work of chaplains but knew virtually nothing of the existence of non-stipendiary ministers.

From within the church NSM may appear a logical develop-ment, with appeals to ecclesiastical precedent and, it has to be said, dissatisfaction with some stipendiary ministers. From outside, however, it may look like a worrying symbol of a church that has lost confidence in its distinctive ministry and in the role of its clergy in the community.

The Clergy's Response

If these are some of the reasons why institutions may welcome the church's ministry, how do the clergy react? In particular, how do they balance the competing expectations of a congregation that wants its ministers to care for it and generate growth within it and a world that wants the church to minister to it on its terms? Faced with such pressure, which is likely to become more intense, the danger is that they will opt for one and ignore the other.

Some may be so attracted to involvement in the world of institutions that they lose contact with the church and congregation from which they come. One of the first signs is when they ignore the distinctively religious activity of the priest's praying for people. The world of work is the 'real' world and the congregation almost a trifling irrelevance. One obvious consequence may be that the priest will so absorb the ethos of the institution that he will soon become indistinguishable from others working within it. The danger then is that, while he may feel that he is contributing something distinctive to the life of that institution, he will have

24

lost the basis of a distinctively priestly ministry and be deluding himself.

More commonly, however, the choice is exercised the other way round. The present attitude of the Church of England is marked by suspicion of institutions and organizations, an emphasis on giving individuals priority over the corporate, and a practical need to build congregations large and committed enough to pay their way. The parish priest is encouraged to respond to expectations from the community on the grounds that, if met, they will serve to build up the congregation. But the balance has swung too far in the direction of ministry to people as potential members of a congregation. Any abandonment of institutions within the parish is not the result of the world becoming disenchanted with the church so much as the church's withdrawal from a difficult but essential activity. It is easy projectively to 'blame' the world for not wanting the church, while all the time the church is itself pulling further and further away from that world.

The activity of ministry necessarily brings no guaranteed reward. This is a commonplace in all thinking about ministry. We argue further, however, that work with those outside the church, especially institutions, is the paradigm of Christian ministry from which all other practices of ministry derive. This is the reverse of what is generally assumed. Ministry is seen first as something done with the people of God which, in some aspects (usually disputed) may also be extended to those outside the church. But without some awareness of the basic paradigm of 'others first', whatever is done within the congregation will prove limited in scope and progressively decline in effectiveness.

But involvement with institutions can be a difficult ministry. Most clergy find ways of coping with the internal life of the church and, after a period, feel reasonably at home there. Playing away from home is tougher. Institutions are strange and confusing. They have complex internal structures, some grasp of which is crucial if any real contribution is to be effective. Yet for the outsider these are mysterious. The priest's feeling of being unsure of his ground, coupled with the awareness that this can be a highly visible area of ministry, which can expose the unwary in

25

embarrassing public positions, leads many clergy to be cautious about the whole approach. Add to that hostility from some of their congregations towards anything that takes them away from time spent with them, and it is an easy move to shift their efforts into building up congregations or a so-called 'enabling' ministry. Institutional involvement can be dismissed because rarely, if ever, will it produce any signs of measurable success.

A Working Theology for Ministry

This option can only be avoided if the Church of England recovers a theological understanding of parochial ministry, rather than unspecific theologies of generalized 'ministry'. Such an understanding will include at least three major elements, which can here be offered only in outline.

First, it will be rooted in a positive approach to creation. Much contemporary Christianity, especially as lived at the congregational level, lacks this awareness. Christians when asked about what difference their faith makes to them respond in terms of different moral behaviour and suggest that to be a Christian might involve adopting a higher ethical code. The world in general is perceived, however vaguely, as a place dominated by evil and redolent with sin, from which the Christian is redeemed. But this attitude is only a half truth. Creation precedes redemption and the biblical stories speak of an original goodness that was not obliterated by the fall and that may be discerned in every dimension of God's world. The world's life, including all that in a secular society, is as a matter of faith set in the context of God the Creator, however much it may also need redeeming.

If God is God, then he is present in the people and institutions of the parishes. By actively involving himself within the wider community of his parish, the priest points men and women (whether Christian or not) to God at work in their world, or at least to the possibility of a transcendent dimension to their world. The presence of a clergyman implies a blessing, in a way which that of a layman cannot. And to bless something is not to bring God to it but to acknowledge his ownership of it. Before clergy can see themselves as agents of redemption they need to become more confident as blessers of creation.

26

Secondly, the theology which undergirds such ministry will spring from an understanding of redemption which is informed by incarnation. Redemption has been achieved through God's involving himself in the ambiguities and messiness of this world's everyday life. If that process is taken seriously by those who follow Christ, then they will often be required to work in similarly messy and ambiguous circumstances. By his active presence, struggling to interpret what is going on in and around him, the priest will witness to God as both creator and redeemer – author and changer.

But thirdly, if such a view of ministry is to sustain some idea of the importance of the congregation, it will have to include awareness of the representative nature not just of the priest but of the church as a whole. There is a godward aspect to the created order and the church is one means by which this is represented. By his presence in secular institutions the priest may focus that aspect, reminding people of that dimension to their lives and to the life of the institution. But when the congregation is at worship it is the whole congregation, which itself may be conceived as an institution, that represents the world to God. Worshippers are not there just for the sake of their individual piety. They bring with them those parts of the world and its life in which they are caught up – family, work, friends, and general concerns. In worship all that world is represented before God.

Curiously it seems that people who would not normally come to a church service are frequently aware of others who are there vicariously on their behalf. The light-hearted 'Say one for me', said to many a churchgoer, may, of course, be no more than a flippant remark. But more often it indicates an instinctive awareness of this representative nature of the congregation, which may be more evident to the non-attender than to the worshippers themselves. But once this fact is perceived, then the monastic adage that work becomes prayer and prayer becomes work is revitalized for the modern world.

With the announcement of the Decade of Evangelism much is already being made of the need to proclaim the gospel, to hold out the possibility of conversion, and to teach the faith. That is wise. But if the Decade is not to result in yet more pressure on clergy to abandon a wider ministry in favour of concentration on

27

enlarging congregations, it needs to be balanced by a recognition that the church also proclaims the gospel by bringing the world to God in prayer and worship.

> God has given the Church of England particular gifts which are well suited to the preaching of the Gospel in these times. We are equipped to face the complexity of our situation because we are not a Church of hard edges. God has worked to keep our borders open . . . Just as we have never divided evangelism from pastoral care, so the Church of England has never separated evangelism from worship.[2]

Ministry by parochial clergy, to individuals and especially to institutions, is crucial to that proclamation. That is not an outdated model of ministry, but one which has an intrinsic pastoral and theological strength for the foreseeable future.

Notes

1. *The Church Times*, 2 November 1990.
2. Robert Runcie in his final presidential address to the General Synod, November 1990.

3

COMMON PRAYER

It is not possible to write about the Church of England without reference to its worship. It has often been said that this church is marked less by particular order or specific doctrine than by its adherence to a form of worshipping – especially the Book of Common Prayer – as its point of joining and sustaining. In this century great attention has been paid to worship and Anglican scholars have been in the vanguard of liturgical study. Parallel to this, however, has been social change which suggests that the idea of a whole people engaged in regular worship has gone for ever. Nevertheless, worship remains a necessity at certain times and places, and, as a consequence, the leaders of the Church of England should ensure that this facet of the church's life is not domesticated and taken away from people in general. David Conner and Stephen Platten, both experienced in creative liturgy in schools, parishes and cathedrals, contribute the main ideas to this chapter.

'If you wish to understand the Church of England, then first you must understand its worship.' This has long been an implicit, and sometimes even an explicit, assumption. Through family likeness the same truth is frequently applied to Anglicanism worldwide. It is a facet of that argument which emphasizes that the Anglican way is not one of dogma and deduction. To be an Anglican is not first and foremost to follow a confessional formula or a code of canon law, although the church does possess some codification. The Church of England is primarily identified by the worship which derives from the 1662 Book of Common Prayer. Even the Thirty Nine Articles do not chiefly define it. In spite of the influence of the Alternative Service Book, and its predecessors Series 1, 2 and 3, many still claim that one will most easily appreciate 'the Anglican way' by attending Evensong in a country church or a quiet eight o'clock celebration of the Prayer Book Eucharist. It is here that the traditional resonances of *ecclesia Anglicana* are instinctively discerned.

The Anglican Ideal?

If these often repeated affirmations contain any truth, however residual, then they reverberate wherever the Church of England contributes something to people's lives. What lies beneath them will also make its mark upon the nature and content of Anglican beliefs. The old Latin tag, *lex orandi, lex credendi* – the rule of prayer is the rule of belief, rings true: doctrine is determined by worship and prayer. To believe and to live as an Anglican is to absorb a culture which extends from the Prayer Book services for marriage and the burial of the dead to that rare occasion when a sovereign is crowned by the Archbishop of Canterbury in Westminster Abbey. It is to find oneself in solidarity with the inchoate religious instincts of the English people. Those who are overtly godly express these week by week in Sunday worship; the majority of the population still does the same on family or national occasions. Worship gives voice to those religious aspirations which, along with other factors, give some sense of identity to 'the people'.

There is still some truth in these assumptions. But they also scarcely disguise a casual romanticism. For, apart from ignoring the degree of secularization within English society, such assertions take no account of the fragmentation and pluralism which now characterize the worship of the Church of England. What exactly is this fragmentation and where do we discover its roots?

The Fragmented Reality

It is now a commonplace that in many busy parishes there are three distinct, often separate, congregations. Incumbents are often distressed throughout their ministry over whether and how to integrate the life of these distinct groupings so that the church in that place retains some sense of unity of purpose. How can the eight o'clock congregation be persuaded to attend the ten o'clock

Sung Eucharist once a month? How might the Evensong faithfuls be encouraged to induct themselves into eucharistic worship? How will the young families, who form the majority of the Sung Eucharist congregation, learn something of these other two traditions? And having asked those questions, the vicar will go on to ask whether he should have asked them in the first place? Does it matter? In the recent past there was a different pattern, by which the faithful might attend an early celebration and later either Matins or Evensong, or even both.

The contemporary dislocation in patterns of attendance at worship extends beyond the busy life of suburban or country parishes. Moving from one village to another in the countryside may expose the peripatetic churchgoer to a kaleidoscopic range of different rites and practices. The Eucharist itself may be that of 1662 (although more likely 1928) or it may be Rite A or Rite B from the Alternative Service Book. If it is Rite A, then the multiplicity of choices is enormous, even within the one printed order. There are 21 Notes to the Rite A Order for Holy Communion, which allow for adjustments. Note 20 is typical:

Hymns, Canticles, the Peace, the Collection and Presentation of the Offerings of the People, and the Preparation of the Gifts of Bread and Wine Points are indicated for these, but if occasion requires they may occur elsewhere.

It is a menu from which the discerning liturgical chef may put together his own desired meal. Rubrics and paragraph numbers become landmarks which replace the prayers which served this purpose for earlier generations.

This phenomenon is by no means restricted to worship in the countryside. A priest recently returned from ten years in the United States of America, where the revised Prayer Book of 1977 is used in a fairly consistent manner throughout the American Church. He was dazzled by the variety and inconsistency which he discovered on four successive Sundays in different inner-London parishes. The first church used Rite A with hymns, in a style which might be defined as 'central Anglican'. The second was celebrating its Harvest Festival and so the Eucharist was supplemented by an extended offertory, in which the members of the congregation were encouraged to bring symbols of their daily

professional work to the altar. The third church had dispensed
with the formal liturgy of the word and replaced it with a number
of choruses, interspersed with homiletic dialogue and with one
reading only. Where standard prayers were used, they were
referred to simply by the paragraph numbers in the Alternative
Service Book. The final church used Rite A in a manner which
corresponded largely with the Roman Catholic *Missa Normativa*
with prayers interjected from that Rite.

This set of experiences was centred entirely on the Rite A
eucharistic order, although the services, both in content and in
feel, often appeared to bear little relationship to each other from
church to church. This marks the abandonment of the earlier
concept of 'common prayer' and consequently represents radical
change in the self-awareness of the Church of England. To return
to our earlier questions, what are the roots of this change and
how self-consciously have they been explored?

The roots are certainly complex and tangled. Some of them
extend into the soil of changing cultural patterns. In the past
twenty years, for example, Evensong as a formal service has
ceased in a large number of parishes. This is apparently because
most people who now attend Church wish to worship only once
on a Sunday and generally that will be in some form of Parish
Communion. Evensong has doubtless suffered through the
influence of television. Where it does survive, it is often sung to
the Order in the 1662 Book of Common Prayer. The echoes of
earlier generations continue to resound. Even so it is a spiritual
pastime of the few, who will rarely have much contact with, or
indeed knowledge of, the contemporary fissiparous eucharistic
traditions outlined earlier. If they feel solidarity with anyone, it is
most likely to be with an earlier generation rather than with the
majority of their present Anglican co-religionists.

But in addition to changing patterns of behaviour, conscious
liturgical adjustments have contributed to this fragmentation.
Earliest of the recent influences here was the 'parish communion'
movement. Although its theological roots go back some fifty
years or more, its impact has been most keenly felt since the
Second World War. The chief aim of the movement was to
restore the Eucharist to the centre of people's Christian lives. It
drew its energy from several, not least the Tractarian, traditions
of the nineteenth century. It has, however, extended well beyond

the bounds of any one party within the Church of England. Furthermore it has largely won its argument. Some form of parish communion almost universally now forms the core of the church's Sunday worship. Alongside the undeniable growth in congregational life which it has brought, it has failed, some would argue, to keep true to the intentions of some of its earliest proponents. The lack of liturgical 'depth' in some places and the introverted and sectarian feel of the Eucharist in other places would not have been effects sought by Gabriel Hebert or Ernie Southcott.

Our concern here, however, is not to analyze these specific points, although each certainly plays its part in weakening the sense of solidarity within the church and between the church and society as a whole, which the concept of 'common prayer' implies. Parish communion has in practice often meant for many churches both the end of Evensong and the beginnings of fragmentation into separate congregations within one parish. It has thus signalled an implicit confirmation of a kind of individualism rather than of a worshipping community under God.

At the same time as the parish communion movement was establishing its hold upon the Church of England, the liturgical movement was generally beginning to make an impact. This movement has been distinctively ecumenical in its development and in its influence. Historical study of ancient liturgies has led to the believed rediscovery of some of the earliest patterns of eucharistic worship. These formulae have been determinative in shaping revised eucharistic rites in all the mainstream churches. In the Church of England this process of revision was more than usually complex. In an attempt to hold together different needs and different understandings of worship, many alternative possibilities have been built into the new liturgies. Nowhere is this more obvious than in the modern language eucharistic order, Rite A. Even before this, however, the roots of fragmentation had become firmly rooted in the fertile ground of the Church of England's parish system. In the late 1960s and early 1970s, the familiar and rather staid and formal looking Book of Common Prayer had been supplanted by a series of pamphlets. With the advent of Rite A and its permissive rubrics, the plethora of different booklets has mushroomed. Common prayer is not what it was.

Recovering Stability

None of the above argument is designed to support moves to return to the Book of Common Prayer. Instead, the aim has been simply to demonstrate the breakdown of the ideal and indeed the practice of common prayer. We need to distinguish between what the Book of Common Prayer represents, in terms of an ecclesiology which opens the church to people and loosely, but firmly, holds that church together, and the language of its rites. Partly because of this confusion the Church of England has too rapidly and casually surrendered an ideal about itself. As a result it has minimized its own particular sense that in worship the church possesses one means of connecting with profound resonances within society. The design of liturgy on this basis specifically reflects a solidarity with all and not just with the overtly pious.

Liturgical reform has also removed too rapidly for many the 'landmarks' which were once albeit dimly recognized by a cross-section of the population as part of their religious heritage. Even the Lord's Prayer is not the same: there is scarcely a more divisive liturgical announcement than when the minister says 'Our Father' and stops. Unlike other churches in English speaking countries (including the Roman Catholic church) the Church of England opted for a radical revision and not for the more conservative form known to many as the Series 2 Lord's Prayer. This means that those who are not regular churchgoers, when attending a marriage or a funeral, will find that the Lord's Prayer, phrases of which they might dredge up from childhood or other memories, is not that which they are now invited to recite. Unnecessary discomfort ensues: another resonance has disappeared; one more sign of welcome and familiarity has been destroyed; solidarity with the wider community through worship is further impaired.

Of course, the charge of romanticism may again be raised. With the apparent eroding of public expressions of folk religion, does any of this solidarity genuinely remain within our society or is such talk merely sentimental? This question moves us on directly to the role of the parish priest in praying and within worship. This has already been briefly discussed in the context of the parochial ministry in Chapter 2 and mentioned implicitly in the new patterns of worship which we have already described. There is an expectation of parish clergy with regard to baptism, marriage and the burial of the dead. The way in which a priest ministers at these times, and the way in which he both constructs and conducts worship, will be of significance for those involved. The latter are usually more than merely those present: there is a knock-on effect through reports of what happened at the service and the gossip which goes on in any community. But beyond these rather obvious expectations lie some more subtle and less easily articulated feelings about the role of the vicar in prayer.

In a suburban parish the local community worker was an ex-Roman Catholic priest, who had left his priestly ministry to marry. He continued to work closely with the Anglican clergy, particularly on the council estate where he was based. He was most concerned that a priest should continue to live on that estate and that he should be seen in clerical collar walking or bicycling along the streets. His argument was not that the people of that estate were especially impressed with him as 'their' priest. More importantly they saw him daily climb the hill to the church to pray. They expected him to do this and in some fashion saw him as doing it on their behalf. They would have had no knowledge of 'the office', its shape, its content or its structure. They would, however, have believed that he was praying: that was his *officium* – 'job', which he did not just for himself or for those who regularly attended the church, but for them. His prayer expressed their un-expressed prayer.

If this is all true in urban and suburban areas, it is still more the case in country areas. Here, as everyone involved in pastoral reorganization soon discovers, each village wants to keep its own vicar. One of the chief functions and duties of that person will be to pray for the people of the parish. He will be the representative person just as much in that sense, as in the sense of being one of the key figures in the village community alongside the publican and the schoolmaster or schoolmistress. This expectation of the parish priest has also been threatened by unavoidable changes in the structure of rural church life. Since early in this century neither finance nor manpower has allowed one incumbent to be provided for one village in many cases. Nevertheless, the belief

35

seems to persist that this was until recently the norm. Now it is possible, for example, in rural Lincolnshire for one priest to be responsible for ten tiny parishes and thirteen church buildings. In seventy square miles of land there are fewer than seven hundred parishioners. It is difficult to know to what extent the felt worshipping presence of the minister is sustained in such an extreme case.

In some rather less pressured circumstances, however, the priest has tried to respond to the expectations placed upon him with regard to prayer and worship. Wherever possible each village will see something of him on each Sunday, or at least on a reliably regular basis. One parish priest with four country parishes was keen to remind all within his cure that he prayed for them and with them daily. Each morning he would tour the four parishes on his moped, tolling the bell at each church. At the fourth church he would stop and say the morning office. Each morning he would say it at a different church. The bell was rung to let all know that prayer was being offered up for the entire community daily. From one angle such behaviour seems eccentric. From another, however, we can discern the idea and ideal of solidarity in offering prayer to God 'sacramentally' in each church in each village. This sacramental understanding of worship is important and directs us to a further point.

Liturgy and Education through Symbol

As it has been a commonplace that Anglican doctrine is determined by its liturgy, so it has also been claimed in the churches that liturgy is an essential arena for Christian education. Despite the contemporary explosion of interest in theology amongst the laity, only a minute proportion of churchgoers attend lectures, complete courses, or attend house groups for study. The point where one can expect to make contact with the greatest number of people throughout the year remains worship. The liturgy has, therefore, increasingly been regarded as an opportunity for Christian teaching. This seems undoubtedly to be one of the causes of that didacticism which prevails within our revised liturgies.

Even a cursory glance through the Alternative Service Book

makes this clear. Prayers are couched in a form intended to press home theological points and little is left to the imagination. The words at the fraction in the eucharistic Rite A are perhaps the supreme example of this tendency. They assume little subtlety in the minds of the congregation, as the priest is instructed to lift and break the bread while saying the words: 'We break this bread to share in the Body of Christ'. Similar points can be made about the revised forms of the occasional offices. In the Te Deum it would appear that even God himself should not be credited with too much certainty about his identity. Worshippers are required to assert the following:

> You are God and we praise you;
> You are the Lord and we acclaim you.

While it may be true that today worship is the one occasion when the Christian community gathers, it is not obvious that the only, or even the main, aim of worship should be to educate. This dimension should not be entirely excluded; but to allow it to become the primary element distorts the nature of worship. There is a profound sense in which worship is one of the few remaining 'non-utilitarian' aspects of human behaviour which is accessible to all.

For that reason it is essential to see worship not as an opportunity to harangue, but rather as an opportunity to articulate our sense of God and our call to offer thanksgiving, praise and contrition. Where that remains the understanding of worship, then once again we shall articulate our solidarity with all people, with consequent blessing for them as well as for the church. Those same elements expected of the priest as he daily prays the office are expected of the entire congregation gathered together in the liturgy of the Eucharist or indeed at Sung Evensong. As the congregation in worship expresses unexpressed religious yearnings on behalf of people, so it becomes a means of drawing all people into a community under God.

This perception implies a particular approach to worship which will by no means concentrate on the words alone. The Eucharist has from earliest times been seen as a drama and not a monologue or even dialogue. *Anamnesis* implies re-enactment. The celebration of the Eucharist is customarily described as the 'eucharistic action'. Through all liturgy this implies motion and the use of symbol. In certain contexts this has meant the stylized drama of a 'High Mass', or in a rather different context the washing of the feet on Maundy Thursday. Particularly in those parts of our society where people are less verbally competent, the significance of movement, of symbol, and of drama will take centre stage. It would be wrong to assume, however, that for the more articulate the same is not true. Indeed, alongside drama, movement and symbol we should place music. In many parts of our society participation within or simply listening to music has replaced the desire to listen to the rhetorical and sometimes stylized orations of the charismatic personalities of religious and political life. Movement and music can often most powerfully express the religious hankering which we share. For they provide a common language.

Articulating Solidarity in God

These arguments place before the church, and especially its clergy, important questions and requirements. By articulating our solidarity in God within our wider world, we shall, through worship, be edified. We shall be built up and that may be the only perspective from which worship can rightly be regarded as utilitarian. Even here any utilitarianism is a derivative of the main *raison d'être* of all liturgy – the articulation of thanksgiving and praise. If people are to articulate a sense of God effectively and thus to be edified, high standards are required from those devising and leading the liturgy. Only worship done well will edify, and as a result participants will unconsciously be educated. Believers will thus be strengthened in their Christian lives and so speak evangelically of the gospel, not necessarily in any explicit fashion but as part of their living the life which is formed through prayer and worship. In that sense, evangelization means to take from worship the grace of God into that wider world, which expects someone daily to offer prayer to God on its behalf.

This crucial activity requires two demanding elements in the life of the clergy and of the church. There is a real sense in which the wider community expects holiness from the clergy. People may find it difficult to articulate exactly what is meant by holiness.

Presumably it will at least mean a visible regularity in prayer. It will mean a commitment to society as a whole and not only to a local gathered congregation. Clergy will also be faced with the subtle task of discovering the best way of ordering worship so that the church remains as open to the community as possible and also continues to articulate its solidarity in God.

It is not clear that this is possible simply on a basis of individual whim or even local preference. The Church of England may need to search afresh to discover what we might mean by 'common prayer' and how it should best be expressed. This does not imply a return to the Prayer Book in a manner called for by some both within and outside the church. Nor does it mean that we can indulge in a nostalgia for a forgotten past. It does, however, require the church to reflect upon the nature of worship and how it relates to the Church of England's understanding of its role. The church is asked to find a 'language' of worship which can become familiar to people in society as a whole and can thus become a means of expressing the shared religious aspirations of the community.

We began with the common assumption that *lex orandi, lex credendi* remains applicable within the Church of England. If that is true, then it may be a clue to our present difficulties in arriving at consensus on doctrinal issues. That simply reflects the fragmentation which exists in the practice of our worship. We cannot expect to regain the unity represented for previous generations by the Book of Common Prayer. Instead, we need to seek for a new and appropriate common understanding of liturgy, prayer and worship which reflects our solidarity in offering to God the hopes and aspirations of all people and not only those of congregations.

'Religion' is probably derived from *ligare* – to bind. Common prayer is a sign of such binding. In being 'common' it may become distantly familiar to those whose contact with the church is sporadic. It thus works to draw the wider world consciously into the orbit of God's love and to articulate the possibility of true community under God. It signals a hope after which many people vaguely hanker and thus answers to deeply-felt need.

4

PUBLIC MINISTERS

Throughout this book the role of the church's public ministers is emphasized. Their representative role and function is reckoned crucial to the life and work of the Church of England. Yet there is a crisis of confidence in that ministry, not so much initiated by the ordained ministers as by questions which arise in synods and the competitive way in which lay activity is sometimes presented. In this chapter some aspects of the clergy's role, whether they are a local minister or a national figure such as the archbishop, are explored. The ideas are based on reflections by John Cox.

Snowy has lived and worked in south-east London as a community worker for the last twenty years. During that time he has become widely known and respected in the community. Recently he was ordained. One evening a man who lives locally but is not a churchgoer cornered him in a pub and wanted to know what to do about his marriage, which was on the rocks. 'Can I have a word with you, vicar', he asked. He knew Snowy's name and had often had a drink with him before. Yet this time he addressed him as 'vicar'.

The Representative Vicar

It was not just a matter of politeness. However unconsciously, the man recognized that ordination had changed the way he thought about Snowy, whatever Snowy may have thought of himself. In some sense, which felt important, it had changed Snowy's status. What he needed at that moment was not Snowy the friend but Snowy the vicar. By using the title 'vicar' he set out the nature of some of his expectations and the basis of his 'contract' with

Snowy before he had even mentioned his particular problem. It is reasonable to postulate that, even though he would never have put it in these terms, the man was looking to Snowy for help with three expectations: first, for someone who represented a way of helping him which included some notion of resource from God; second, for an official church person (not just a Christian); and thirdly, for someone who was trustworthy, whose help and advice he could treat as authoritative.

For Snowy's part, if he was to make the best use of this sudden opportunity, he needed to be able to acknowledge and work with these expectations and not merely respond, as he would previously have done, at the personal level of a Christian friend. The man was not looking for a neighbour or a community worker. The skills which Snowy possessed in these roles might ultimately be involved. But the distinctive contribution he could make at that moment was founded on his being a vicar.

For most people, anyone who wears a dog collar is either a vicar or a bishop. The world is essentially divided into 'vicars' and 'non-vicars'. That the local vicar shares the bishop's authority is hardly grasped. A vague notion of hierarchy is probably carried in the popular mind. In a recent dispute in Yorkshire over whether a horse should be allowed to graze in a churchyard, the local protesters displayed on television a neat sense of hierarchy. Having taken the issue to the Archbishop of York and not got what they wanted, they avowed that they would take it 'to the man above him – the Archbishop of Canterbury' and even, if that failed, the pope. The vicar works in the local setting, the bishop in a wider context, and the archbishop in the widest of all. All other ecclesiastical distinctions are, for most people, a mystery and largely irrelevant. Women deacons, for example, are 'vicars': 'I see they're making women vicars now.'

But such ignorance does not indicate failure to recognize proper distinctions. The church has concentrated its debate on the ordination of women largely around the cultic aspect – priesthood and the presidency of the Eucharist. In doing so it has focused on something significant but has not given adequate consideration to the range of ministry that women do, and are seen, to exercise. Those who call them vicars acknowledge this. Whatever the theological and liturgical understanding of women currently ordained as deacons, and whatever the legal niceties about whether they can or cannot be team vicars, the observable fact is that they can be and are representative figures. That is why they are appropriately greeted as vicars.

The vicar represents the church, not only the local church but the church at large. This simple fact is hardly touched by the church's internal concerns about every member ministry and its current efforts to avoid clericalism, however necessary they may be within their own context. The role of institutional representative is an appropriate and distinctive one. By failing to appreciate this fact, or attempts to escape from it, clergy too quickly relinquish a key understanding of a significant part of their ministry. The church, too, thereby fails to grasp opportunities for engagement with the society around it.

Such a view assumes a particular understanding of the Church of England and its ordained ministry. Whatever the shortcomings in practice, and whatever complementary patterns there need to be, the concept of the vicar in a parish church is not an irrelevant historical accident. It remains an important pattern for the Church of England in fulfilling its mission. The concept of 'parish' refers to more than a geographical location and a physical presence (a local parish church and an incumbent). It denotes a quality of potential relationship between the church and society in general, specifically between clergy and people other than members of a congregation. It is, therefore, an idea in the mind, not only of the church (where it sometimes seems attenuated today) but of people at large. And such 'ideas in the mind' usually come to life when people engage with other people, in this case parishioners with a vicar.

For example, when in 1990 Ian Gow was murdered by the IRA, two figures noticeably appeared in the media: the local vicar and the local bishop. They were obviously in touch with the widow. Their appearances not only provided public assurance that care was being offered to the family; they also functioned as symbols of reassurance to a wider community and even the country. The murder of a Member of Parliament, himself a representative figure, stirred up outrage. It also aroused a general feeling of threat to security. Factual explanations of who may have planted the bomb and how it may have been made did not relieve the overwhelming sense of mystery and awe, which needed specifically to be handled. In Northern Ireland, where religion is a more significant facet of public life than in the rest of the United Kingdom, however repetitive statements seem to be when tragedies occur, this expectation is not exhausted. The clergy remain key people in the task of articulating the anguish of a community. Both in England, with its less overt religious behaviour, and in Ireland, ministers are believed to be able to handle what is mysterious and terrible, especially death. They represent God and the institution of the church, both of which it is hoped might be able to face and handle the intrusion of chaos. The vicar and bishop were representative figures: the vicar standing for reassurance at the individual and local level, the bishop at the individual and national level, and both at the level of some undefined 'beyond', the transcendent.

Being a representative is a central aspect of the ordained minister's role. Within a community, however that is defined, the vicar represents the church, which is the institution in society that handles the things of God. But being a representative of the institution is a particular role in a range of roles. It is not the same thing as being the only one who carries out its task. There is always a danger that the idea of representation can become a justification for monopolizing. The vicar may be tempted to take entirely upon himself or herself the work of the local congregation in its task of living out and bearing witness to the things of God. The idea of ministry then becomes understood as what the vicar does, not only legitimately as a representative of the church but falsely in the place of everyone else.

Such lack of clarity about the nature of representation can produce a distorting clericalism, which is today more frequently condemned than it is in practice found. It can also, however, by a process of overreaction, lead to a pseudo-egalitarianism whereby all ministry is considered the same and no one is allowed to be believed to possess a specifically representative role. There is a form of anticlericalism which is found within the church rather than among those to whom the church offers its ministry. In some places this is justified as 'every member ministry'. Yet where those who are in a legitimate position of authority fail to exercise it, space is left for a struggle for power, which is legitimized as

'Christian', 'primitive' or 'biblical'. This phenomenon can some-times be seen in a parish. It also, however, features more widely as, for instance, in the problematic relationship between the General Synod and the bishops. There are problems around the authority of bishops in that setting which remain unresolved. When it suits, boundaries between bishops, clergy and laity are blurred under the head of 'Synod Member': when it does not, there is usually a call for a vote by houses.

When the man in the pub called Snowy 'vicar', it was he, not Snowy, who determined the representative role. The church, by ordaining Snowy, assigned him authority to represent it, and so for many people, also to represent God. The man was acknowledging this and, by invoking Snowy's role as 'vicar', he was making it become genuine in practice. Recognizing that he or she is such a representative is essential for every ordained minister, but especially for the clergy of the Church of England. For them this representation can never be solely to a congregation or even to people with residual Anglican belief. The minister functions as a religious person in the setting of folk or common religion, which happens to take Christian form. What really counts, therefore, in thinking about the structure and ordering of the church's ministry is not only its own self-awareness but also the extent to which that perception is shared by the members of the community and society around.

The Vicar in the Community

In a reasonably stable community which draws upon its historical roots, the local church and vicar may be perceived as accessible and dependable. But in the more fragmented and pluralist communities of contemporary society, especially in the urban setting, it is less obvious that one institution (the local Church of England church) can fulfil this function for the community at large. In some areas, although only in practice a few, adherents to faiths other than Christianity are in the majority and the mosques and gurdwara may be looked to rather than the parish church. That context simply assigns the parish church and the vicar a different task, for which, however, clergy and laity of the Church of England are as yet mostly unprepared. More broadly, alienation from society and distrust of its institutions may characterize the position of an increasing number of people. Any religious or other symbols of dependency then become a focus of anger.

The 1980s have seen a concerted attempt by the Church of England to address the way it relates to those parts of our society which feel most alienated from dependable symbols. With an ever widening gap between the life chances and opportunities of three quarters of the population and those of the less fortunate quarter (principally occupying the inner cities), *Faith in the City* has provided the basis for another examination of the way the urban underclass has rejected nearly all forms of institutional religion.

As we enter the 1990s there is little evidence that within the Church of England any major shift in understanding how to address these issues has taken place. The Roman Catholic Church has strengthened its position in many inner city communities. We may be learning again that the voice of protest and dissent in English society may identify more closely with the Free Churches or the Roman Catholic Church than with the Church of England. Nevertheless, the Church of England has, against the odds, remained in the inner city areas chiefly because of the dedication of its clergy. The parochial system, for all its faults, has ensured that clergy still for the most part live within the communities they serve. In speaking with and for those communities, therefore, the church is heard to be speaking with and for the disadvantaged.

But social and community concern alone does not make the church. Nor does it give the clergy significance within the life of the community. That seems to be acquired because the clergy 'stand for God', and in standing for God communicate 'the ways of God to men and women'. Obviously speaking an esoteric, theological jargon is not communicating God. But neither is activity alone, however concerned and well-meaning. Clergy need the ability to interpret the day to day lives and events of women and men in the light of the gospel, and to do so whether those lives are lived in inner city or suburbia, estate or village. It is what people ultimately expect of the clergy, and failure to articulate a theological interpretation of life is to falter in the task for which clergy have been ordained. Such a failure to attempt to speak

45

about God is not only to let down the church; it also results in the minister so disappointing basic human expectations that he or she is unable to engage with people at depth on any topic. We should have reached the end of our nervousness about speaking of God.

The concept of the vicar as representative has a long tradition. But this has been expressed in other terms and sometimes in limited ways. For example, the priest may be spoken of as the representative of God to people and of people to God. The context for this has most often been liturgical and specifically in relation to sacramental acts, which are on behalf of the particular people of God. What, however, is in danger of being overlooked is that these are points where the vicar's representative role within the church and that generated by the expectations of others, intersect. The parallel with the convergence of eternity with this world in the sacraments is obvious. Thus the vicar taking babies into his arms to baptize them may be reminiscent of Jesus welcoming the children and hence represent God's openness to all. The point would be emphasized if these words were restored as a baptism lection: 'Suffer the little children to come to me, and forbid them not. For of such is the Kingdom of Heaven' (Mark 10.14). Taking bread, giving thanks, breaking and sharing it at the Holy Communion, is also a representative action. But the emphasis in modern liturgies is on the priest who presides as the whole body of the church offers, consecrates and shares. Yet such development need not diminish the importance of representation, unless the connection between the internal life of the church and the context in which it is set is dissolved.

The Sunday morning car-washer may call to his neighbour as she goes down the street to church, 'Don't forget to say one for me.' Worshippers do not merely praise and confess and intercede as so many individuals engaged in private acts of religion. They, too, become representative figures for their neighbours and the remark is not always an idle phrase for passing an awkward moment. It articulates a sense that in communities some people are called upon to represent others in their involvement with the things of God. The vicar is manifestly one such a representative figure. He or she, however, functions in this way not only for a wider community than the membership of the church but also for the congregation.

The saying of the daily offices illustrates this contention. Even when alone, the vicar begins, 'O Lord, open *our* lips'. He is taking part in a public, corporate act, not a private one, in his representative role. A TV programme some years ago presented the lone vicar saying the morning office in an empty church as a symbol of the desperate plight of the church. The producer had failed to take the representative notion properly into account. But so do many clergy. They are not required to say the offices primarily as part of their own spiritual development, although it clearly relates to their personal discipline. The requirement ensures that the pastor's prayers are always for those others whom he or she represents.

In considering vicars as representatives of the community there is the danger of their presuming too much and so becoming paternalistic. In considering the vicar as representative of the congregation there is the danger of monopolizing ministry and of the congregation colluding in an acquiescent passivity. There are dangers, too, in being the one who represents God. But, following the example of Jesus himself, it has not been part of the Christian way to try and escape misunderstandings rather than risk opportunities for working with people.

Vocation and Selection

To represent God is not a position to seize: it is given by appointment only. The idea of vocation, the calling of God and of the church to the individual to take on this role, is crucial. But the gap between the role assigned and the person who holds it can appear to be so great as inevitably to expose clergy to the charge of hypocrisy. There is nothing new in this. It has always been necessary to affirm, for example, that personal inadequacies do not invalidate the effect of a sacrament. Nevertheless, to speak for God not only lays a person open, in their own eyes and in the eyes of others, to their unworthiness: it can also reveal an actual incongruence that diminishes the effectiveness of the role. This is one key reason why clergy are required to be people of personal faith and spiritual depth (holiness) and why prayers are offered at their ordination for God's grace to fulfil their calling. Holiness is not a matter of being 'holier than thou'. It is sharing in the knowledge and awareness of God in a way that pervades the whole person, so that others find the clergy to be sufficiently trustworthy and accessible ways to the reality of God. One of their representations is to be holy people.

If the Church of England is to have ministers who can recognize and attempt to carry such a role, with all its personal, spiritual and intellectual demands, then the selection and training of future clergy is a critical issue. Over the last generation or so a vocation has been understood almost entirely in terms of the individual's inner sense of the call of God. Biblical accounts of God's call have been interpreted in this way. The church has responded to the individual call by confirming it or not. Recently there has been a renewed plea for a more balanced understanding of vocation in which the individual and the church participate more equally. The church is involved in the calling of the individuals and not solely in the testing of their call. This approach finds its biblical justification in an interpretation of the call of leaders, prophets and disciples within a corporate setting rather than a purely individual one.

But this trend also relates to the desire in many quarters for local congregations to play a larger part in the prompting and discernment of vocations. This creates the danger that too much significance might be given to local theological understandings of ministry, and conflict might therefore increase with the national selection process. There is always a touch of 'them' and 'us' between the local and national selection. The sponsoring bishop, who is supposed to represent both aspects of the procedure, is then expected to resolve any problems which arise. This is a naturally human way of behaving and, therefore, not surprising. We need, however, in dealing with such tendencies to be able to respond not only organizationally but, more importantly, with a theological perspective. It is, therefore, both significant and potentially revolutionary that the bishops have recently endorsed an approach to theological education which is local (i.e. determined in style and educational approach by the college or course) but which is monitored centrally by the Advisory Board of Ministry. The balance of 'local' (college or course) and 'central', however, is not maintained merely by structural arrangements. The core questions around which criteria are established concern the nature of the church and its ministry, specifically the Church of England.

Each training institution has in its submission to answer three questions. The first demands attention to the idea of the Church of England and its distinctive ministerial requirement: 'What ordained ministry does the Church of England require?' The second addresses the task of the college or course, namely education: 'What is the shape of the educational programme best suited for equipping people to exercise this ministry?' Finally, the continuing selection procedure is emphasized: 'What are the appropriate means of assessing suitability for the exercise of this ministry?'[1]

The overall shift is clear: some understanding of the church – and specifically its institutional nature – is the prerequisite for the study of its ministry. The same theological theme needs to run through the selection process. This is not to plead that the church should be more centralized in a bureaucratic sense, but that it should be true to its nature as a church rather than as a federation of congregations.

Both discernment and selection depend at some point upon notions that there are publicly acknowledgeable qualities appropriate to the role to be carried out. Intuition (inspiration) has its place in the process. But there is also the need for some broadly agreed criteria in the selection of clergy. The currently accepted criteria remain broadly appropriate, but greater emphasis needs to be given to the qualities which are called for in those who undertake an institutional representative role, and who can make best use of the opportunities that this role offers.

Two aspects are of particular significance: that personal spirituality and integrity which have been described above as 'holiness', and the intellectual ability to fulfil the interpretative function, which is so important in a representative figure. This does not mean a purely academic ability, but the ability of applied intelligence which can perceive and handle connections across situations, activities and concepts, interpreting them in the light of theological understanding. The clergy in the best Anglican tradition are to be marked by 'thoughtful holiness'.

There is a dynamic relationship between the interpretative and

49

the representative roles and they draw together ideas of nearness and distance. Biblical accounts of the prophets in both the Old and New Testaments stress that effective interpretation does not merely describe a situation. It seeks to establish a critique by which it can be judged. For this a certain distance between the interpreter and the situation is required. One long-standing reason for appointing clergy to serve in parishes where they have not been brought up or lived in the immediate past is that it provides just such distancing. In this regard the current assessment of the Non-Stipendiary Ministry needs to be considered very carefully. Reports of the experience of NSMs in the parish context, and even more so of those who see themselves as Ministers in Secular Employment in the work-place, indicate that it is chiefly this lack of perceived distance which presents difficulties. This is another instance of a difference in perception between the church and its thinking about ministry and those who look to it for such care. Moves towards Local Ordained Ministry, which are already beginning to occur, will compound the problem.

Conclusion

The role of the vicar in the parish remains a particularly appropriate concept for the ordained ministry in the Church of England, given its continuing task. There has been and will be change in precisely how this role is perceived. But in the end these people, however they may relate to others and collaborate with them in ministry, have to be able to acknowledge the use made of them as a focus of expectation. However unreasonable this may appear to the vicar, it seems natural to the other person. Whatever his churchmanship or assumptions about ministry, the vicar will without fail find himself in this role in a series of contexts, both within and outside the church. In so doing he is being truly a clergyman in the Church of England.

Nevertheless it has to be recognized that numbers of ordinands are emerging from situations where ministry is understood in quite other terms. These candidates may bring commitment and experience of renewal. But the aim of selection is to ensure that all candidates are open to what will be required of them within the church as it is. This is not a matter of being able to live with people with varying churchmanship or different theological understandings. Ordinands and ministers will soon enough encounter these. Openness is being able to acknowledge that whatever one's personal spirituality and pilgrimage, an ordained minister has to be able and willing to bear the expectations of others, confusing as these may be; prepared to learn what it is to carry a role in people's lives which one can only dimly perceive; and capable of appreciating that the church, whatever shape this may have in one's own mind, is for many people an institution to which they look. Snowy's friend, with his instinctive awareness that the relationship between him and Snowy had changed through the latter's becoming a vicar, has more to teach the church about its ministry than may often be realized by ministers, lay and ordained, in the contemporary Church of England.

Note

1. *Education for the Church's Ministry*. London, ACCM, 1988.

5
THE ELUSIVE CENTRE

Most discussions of authority in the church originate in theories of order or institutional life. While these questions are not unimportant, the experienced problem of authority, whether that of an archbishop, bishop or vicar, is created more by people's expectations than by theories. How these two dimensions are to be held together is a critical question for the continued ministry of the Church of England. Its innate pragmatism prevents it seeking resolution in theory; its claimed catholicity inhibits it from adopting simple solutions to these complex issues. This chapter considers the nature of such authority, looking especially at what is expected from bishops, especially the Archbishop of Canterbury. The ideas have been generated by Graham James.

One of the characteristics of English institutions is their elusiveness. Their centre is sometimes difficult to find, although the fibres of their web are so extensive that it seems there must be one. In our pattern of government these fibres link Downing Street, Parliament, Buckingham Palace, Whitehall and local authorities. In succeeding administrations the web's centre may seem to change, and other bodies (the trade unions, for example) may be drawn into the web for a time before ejection, since they do not really belong. Even at a time when there seems a powerful centre in the web of government, its dispersed character remains.

Locating the Centre

The ancient universities are even more enigmatic and elusive, as is well illustrated by the old story of the American visitor who, having been shown all the colleges in Oxford, still wanted to know where the University was. The Church of England displays the same institutional model and in so doing it mirrors other English institutions. Its structure of authority is dispersed. Wherever you examine the system, this quality prevails. Therein lies its elusiveness and the reason why almost every statement about it requires qualification.

Those who propose a naive prophetic model for the contemporary church are likely to consider this elusive quality a fundamental flaw in the Church of England. How can it preach an uncomfortable gospel to the nation when it is so embedded within it that it seems indistinguishable from the tents of ungodliness? But no church, if it is interacting with its society, can guarantee that it will never inadvertently say, 'Peace, peace, where there is no peace'. But that risk cannot be used to dismiss casually the positive facets of links between church and culture. Indeed, in the emerging churches in other parts of the world inculturation is one of their aims. Many African and Asian churches, for example, have their origins in European missions and are now actively seeking their indigenous forms of organization and structure. This is not merely a matter of forms of worship but also of how the church structures itself in a style which is recognizably indigenous but at the same time publicly Christian.

The Church of England has the same problem, although it also has a longer history of struggling with it. It is inculturated into a peculiar English culture. On reflection we can reasonably claim that what can be its indigenous strength has sometimes been a mistaken export. Outside England institutional elusiveness on the English model can be simply bewildering. But in England its day is not yet done, unless the Church of England has finally separated itself from its environment – something which manifestly has not happened.

Some time ago a cheque for £10 made out to 'The Church of England' was sent to Lambeth Palace. In its small way it neatly presented the problem of locating the Church of England. Who should get the money? Was it the Church Commissioners, the General Synod, the Archbishop of Canterbury, perhaps even the House of Bishops? Or would it have been theologically correct to divide it among the twenty-seven million or so who have been baptized in the Church of England? This trivial example illuminates the same dilemma which arises when people, anxious for authoritative teaching on some issue, ask, 'Where does the Church of England stand?'. Is it reasonable to quote a resolution of the General Synod in reply, or say what the Archbishop of Canterbury thinks, or describe the policy of the Church Commissioners?

The Centralizing Tendency

Despite this enduring characteristic, there is today a growing sense that the Church of England's structure of elusive dispersed authority is gradually giving way to new forms of centralized decision making. The influence of the so-called 'centre' is strongly felt, even if difficult to locate. The payment of the clergy from a central fund has perhaps been the strongest sign of 'centre' and has reduced that sense of independence which the existence of glebe, endowment and tithe once confirmed in the parish clergyman. Where, in Parson Woodforde's diary, for example, do we find him longing for diocesan support for his ministry, for his bishop to 'give a lead', or any acknowledgement of a centre apart from Weston Longueville parish church?

Parson Woodforde, however, also lived in a world where it took weeks for him to learn of the storming of the Bastille. Now any idea of what is local must include the way in which it is constantly penetrated by a consciousness of a wider world. The Church of England's web is still woven with most of the fibres directed towards the local, not least through the continued significance of its parish churches. But it now needs coherent representation on other scales too. Parts of the web which fell into decay in the eighteenth century – Convocation, for example, the only national representative body, ceased to meet from 1717 – today possess renewed power and have altered in shape.

Weston Longueville received its most famous vicar through the patronage of Woodforde's Oxford college, where he was ordained as a fellow. Bishops, both the bench and his diocesan, were incidental to his life and ministry. They were certainly not looked upon as centralizers who had either the capacity or desire to become involved in local parish life. The idea that the bishops

54

would jointly establish a national system for selecting ordinands would have been unthinkable. And this would not just have been because distance and the difficulties of travel militated against it. The idea was culturally unimaginable; not just a practical problem.

Yet since 1945 the Church of England has had such central selection which encourages in the clergy a sense of joining an organized profession, even though anyone expecting a rational career structure is soon disappointed. The new patronage procedures have yet to be fully tested. But it is noticeable that while giving the parish representatives more power, the system eventually hands disputed patronage to the bishop, and ultimately to the archbishop, which confirms the sense of centralized appointments. The creation of the office of Clergy Appointments' Adviser substantiates this shift. Even the parish priest's car loan comes from a central fund administered by the Church Commissioners. Whereas the self-employed National Insurance stamp used to be a small symbol of the clergy's continuing independence, they, like others, are now integrated into the PAYE and NHI systems. This sense of the 'centre' is not confined to the clergy, although they were possibly the first to feel its impact. Massive increases in parish share or quota have made many laity more aware and even suspicious of a creeping bureaucracy.

The above is a description, not a moan. There has certainly been centralization of resources and administration, much of it inevitable in a modern world and some to the benefit of the church. The hideous inequalities in remuneration of clergy, for example, were a major scandal, since they were unrelated to levels of work or responsibility. It is not individual parts of the modern system that are the problem. The package as a whole creates a sense that the Church of England possesses a 'centre' where decisions are made and power resides. It affects work in the parishes, but the vicar and his congregation cannot penetrate its mysteries. When we add to this trend the emergence and first years of activity of the General Synod, we have a commanding and sometimes almost imperious sense of 'centre'.

But to say all this is not to locate it. For it is one of the oddities of life that the centre of power always seems to exist elsewhere and the nearer someone comes to thinking they have found it, the more distant it becomes. The bureaucrat who experiences a sense of impotence in Church House may begin to believe that power actually lies in Lambeth Palace. Yet in reality most of the significant decisions which affect the church's life are not taken nationally or centrally, but at the diocesan and parish level. Indeed some of the most important, such as those affecting its role in education, occur outside its formal structures.

The Prominence of the Synod

There is, however, one pervading assumption that seems to be becoming stronger. This is that this 'centre' subsists in the General Synod. The media may contribute to this belief, but it is not of their creation. The Synod's members sometimes seem to believe it themselves. This error is pardonable. The General Synod has caught the media's attention in a way that few would have predicted. The quality of its debates is rarely inferior to those in Parliament. Frequently they are better informed and always they are more courteous to opposing viewpoints. Because it is a legislative assembly, when it acts legislatively it has teeth. Yet it would be an arid body if its workings were restricted to ecclesiastical legislation alone. The debate on *The Church and the Bomb*, for instance, raised in a public forum an issue in the early 1980s which concerned the nation, yet which Parliament either could not or would not at that time explore in a temperate way. The television coverage of that debate generated a profile for the General Synod which has since been sustained.

Yet it is now more negatively critical. Part of the reason for this shift must be that a body designed to be a legislative assembly begins to act upon its legislative instincts in areas which are not susceptible to legislation. The unhappy debate on sexual morality in November 1987 showed both the Synod's discomfort in doing what it did and its inability to stop itself in full course and prevent itself giving law the upper hand over grace. A further danger, which is also a weakness, in a body which perceives itself as the central authority in the church is that it will attempt to gobble up competition. This tendency is observable during the rituals of Question Time, when the Church Commissioners, the House of

Bishops, the Archbishop of Canterbury and the Synod's own boards and councils are called to account, even in matters outside their (and the Synod's) authority.

These tensions derive from the fact that the Church of England's structure is determined by traditions of office rather than by logically consistent systems of government – hence its organizational elusiveness. It is the product of English history and its office holders represent continuities in the life of both Church and nation. The General Synod by contrast, although having its origins in the Convocations, represents a radical discontinuity. It was created as a result of a belief in the virtues of participative government. But generally the Church of England does not proceed in this way. Bodies emerge and accumulate functions and are theologically justified after the event. Hooker's *Law of Ecclesiastical Polity*, for example, did not offer a programme for the creation of a church. It was an attempt to make theological and legal sense of what the Church of England had become.

Within the synodical system traditional sources of authority in the Church of England are brought into association with elected representatives, whose authority is derived from their electors. In the Deanery Synod, for example, the joint chairmen are the Rural Dean, appointed by the Bishop, and the Lay Chairman, elected by the Lay members. Thus the clergy are represented by an episcopal appointee and not by someone elected by themselves. In the General Synod part of the fascination is the way in which appointees (e.g. the bishops) sit in the same chamber as elected clergy and laity – the Lords and Commons in a single chamber. But this is also the reason for Synod's occasional bewilderment with itself and its ability to baffle outsiders.

The Role of the Archbishop

In complete contrast with the General Synod the bishops, both individually and as a body, are part of an unspoken network of interrelationships at the heart of English society, which is hard to define. In an age in which the clergy are inclined to blur roles, usually so as not to diminish the importance of the laity, it is also a network which needs acknowledging, if the distinctive ministry of the Church of England to those outside its committed membership is to survive. But by the same token we must not expect the church to be immune from contemporary changes in the character of this network. Compared with a generation ago, the profile and prestige of diocesan bishops has declined. By contrast the profile of the Archbishop of Canterbury has been heightened, so much so that the bishops are now sometimes viewed as lesser versions of his role. The new archbishop, for example, was reported as having car-phones and fax machines in order to keep in touch with the bishops. So far as we can see, the report was not questioned, which suggests that the idea was not felt by those observing the church or by the bishops themselves to be at all strange. The public significance of bishops in their own right is determined either by media skills, as with the Bishops of Oxford and Edinburgh, or with opinions considered at variance with those of their colleagues, as with the Bishop of Durham.

This development in the Church reflects changes which have also occurred in the style of government. The Prime Minister is frequently regarded as the authoritative voice of government. Now twice a week he is subject to questions in the House of Commons on every subject, regardless of the specific responsibilities of departmental ministers. Cabinet ministers are widely thought to be implementing policies rather than forming their own.

Margaret Thatcher was in office throughout most of Robert Runcie's time as Archbishop of Canterbury. For whatever reason, both of them were the focus of that particular concentration upon leaders, whether in church, state, industry or sport, which marked the 1980s. Such changes are not easily reversible. One effect has been to add to the expectations located in the Archbishop of Canterbury. Focal, representative figures have become more prominent, but at the expense of other representatives of the same institution. For example, a Member of Parliament complained that the Church of England had been virtually silent on the problems of embryo research when legislation was being considered. Yet the Archbishop of York, and other bishops, had made weighty speeches in the House of Lords. The Archbishop of Canterbury, however, had not then made his views known. The assumption was clear: until the Archbishop of Canterbury had declared his mind, the Church of England had not addressed the issue.

The higher the profile of the central representative figure, the more is expected of him or her. The Archbishop of Canterbury has preached at services for disasters such as the Marchioness tragedy and the Hungerford massacre, as well as for those which took place in or near his own diocese – Zeebrugge and Deal. The memorial service for the victims of the King's Cross fire was appropriately held at St Pancras Parish Church and led by the local area bishop. It went largely unreported. The incident was as serious as the others, but the nation's mourning – a natural consequence of such blanket and intimate coverage of these disasters – seemed not to be handled so well at a national level.

Here we move into dangerous territory for the Church of England and for its leaders. It may be deluding itself by thinking it is handling the nation's experience, helping to affirm its identity or cope with its sense of loss. If it does this uncritically, the leap is made to a slick justification of the status quo and the church's established role. Yet there continue to be signals that it is performing this task and that, as might be expected, it is felt to have disappointed people when some think it fails. A mythology has already sprung up around the service at St Paul's Cathedral at the end of the Falklands' campaign. Yet this is only because there these generalized expectations were handled by the church with the only resources it possesses – those of the Christian gospel. This almost enforced engagement of life and gospel as much (if not more) by choice of society as of the church, is what makes the Church of England's ministry potentially powerful.

Such a church cannot merely add a religious gloss to local or national occasions. Nor can it stand for the goodness of religion. Its gospel is that of Jesus Christ. Indeed, even the undiscerning are now beginning to recognize that religion is not necessarily good in itself. The fear of militant Islam or fundamentalist Christianity both makes some nervous about religion and causes them to acknowledge that its place in human life cannot be disregarded. The Church of England's place in English national life is a recognition of the significance of religion. But this also is a means of conceding the dangers as well as the merits of faith. The Church of England interprets. Even a secularized society needs somebody to undertake that task.

One of the minor signs that this function is recognized is found in the number of charities, institutions and secular organizations which seek association with the Archbishop of Canterbury. They invite his patronage, or a visit or at least a message. Association with the Church of England in secular Britain does not appear to be the deadening influence we are led to believe. Behind the formal request may lie a barely recognized desire for the Archbishop and his church to make sense of religious bewilderment. Archbishop Runcie was once invited to address a large body of bankers. The group, which met regularly, realized that over the previous decade nobody from outside the political, educational or commercial world had addressed them. They felt they needed to recognize people's spiritual aspirations too and to be more informed about the religious movements in our society. Even such a hard-headed commercial body discerned that religion remains a formative influence upon people's decisions, lifestyles and, no doubt, their desire for loans and capacity to repay them. They did not seek access to whatever knowledge or wisdom the Church of England might have through the General Synod, its Board for Social Responsibility or any church institution or organization, but through a person who represented to them the values and tradition of the Church of England and who could be critical about religion whilst committed to a religious view of life.

That invitation, as with so many, was not a request to evangelize, but to interpret. The leaders of the Church of England – especially the Archbishop – are trusted as religious people who might be able still to offer a critical understanding of contemporary religion. That is a distinctive role and one which needs cherishing in an age beset both by fundamentalism and continuing secularizing trends. Whether it can be sustained in an age in which we are consistently reminded that England is multi-cultural and religiously pluralist is often questioned. Yet that pluralism is limited in range and often overestimated. Even in areas where it is most in evidence the Church of England's institutional character may be of assistance in creating harmony where discord threatens.

In 1989, in the wake of problems following the publication of Salman Rushdie's *The Satanic Verses*, a group of senior Muslim leaders in this country met with the two Archbishops and the Bishop of Bradford, and one or two others. The Muslims had a high doctrine of the Church of England's place in the country's social structure, much greater than most Anglicans would attribute to it. Yet for most British Muslims this is not the result of what they have read in books but what they have experienced in this country after living here for many years. The Church of England's primary representative figures can still make the links – new ones, such as with the Muslim leadership – which enable it to discharge its responsibilities within the nation's life. Establishment need not be self-interested.

Personalized Centres

Therefore, if the Church of England has a 'centre', this will never be the bureaucratic focus of the institution, wherever that is located. The centre is the place where its primary representative figures interact with parallel figures in politics, law, the arts, education, industry and commerce. Such a centre is, like the authority of its leading figures, dispersed. At present, for instance, such distribution can be seen in the bishops and in the growing significance of our cathedrals. When the centre of the church is rediscovered to lie within its representative offices rather than in any elected body or electoral system, people will recover confidence in their own roles, whether as clergy or laity, and that confidence will be registered in the parishes.

Recourse to the Scriptures for a blue print for the contemporary church is doomed to failure. The diversity of the primitive Church is well recognized, though its pluriform ethical and doctrinal basis is a less congenial fact to admit. Yet there is an illuminating aspect for our theme in the life and ministry of Jesus, which has been notably explored by W. H. Vanstone.[1] For Jesus, 'going up to Jerusalem' – to the centre of Judaism – always has some foreboding. His teaching ministry takes place locally, away from centres of importance and influence, and even within Galilee an important town like Sepphoris does not get a mention, though many of the smaller surrounding hamlets do. But when he finally comes to Jerusalem he ceases to be as active as hitherto. His role is transformed into that of the one who reveals God's activity and grace by his style of acceptance of what is done to him. The teaching office and the saving activity can never be separated. But the example of Jesus in Jerusalem before Pilate, Herod and the crowd is one in which who he was and what he taught were blended in what others did to him rather than in what he said to them. In the light of its elusive centre, that is a model which the Church of England's leadership must explore.

Note
1. *The Stature of Waiting.* London, Darton, Longman & Todd, 1982.

6
COMMON GROUND

A delicate relationship continues to exist between people in general and the Church of England. One point of contact which illuminates this connection is found in the cathedrals of England, which have discovered in recent years a new liveliness and public significance. The material for this chapter originates from the experience of two theologians who have worked in different cathedrals – Christopher Lewis in the ancient cathedral at Canterbury and Stephen Platten at the smaller parish church cathedral in Portsmouth.

'Are you a Londoner?' she asked. 'No, no, I come from Hampstead,' he replied. 'Where do you come from?' 'Oh, I come from London; I live in Woking.' Both conversations are plausible. For some it is a compliment to be addressed as a Londoner, for others it is an insult. It all depends.

Visitors to Cathedrals

Human gatherings, groups and institutions are notoriously difficult to define and the church is no exception. Both from outside and from within there is disagreement about where the church, especially the Church of England, begins and ends. Who is a member and who is not? For whom does the church exist? How do the expectations of different groups of people and how does the present practice of the church shape and unconsciously define its limits?

An approach to these questions can be made through the particular case of cathedrals. Many who would rarely find themselves associated with Christian worship clearly feel that cathedrals are part of the English way of life. The spire of Salisbury, the towers of Durham or Canterbury, the dome of St

63

Paul's, even Hereford's *mappa mundi* are regarded as national property. Reactions to any proposal to charge for entry into some cathedrals emphasize this point. Cathedrals are assumed to be for all to visit, whatever their religious convictions. Those responsible for cathedrals may see this affection as both a blessing and a curse. On the financial level, visitors mean income; to some extent they help keep stone on stone. On the human level, sightseers give a cathedral life and vigour. Tourist agencies and advisers now talk of 'interpreting' cathedral buildings. What messages do the buildings convey and how can people be helped to experience them? Yet there are dangers. A 'ministry of welcome' may appear mercenary, a thinly disguised way of asking for an entrance fee. The crowds may make it impossible for some people to find the space and peace for which they have come. Signs which are designed to be helpful may appear directive or even forbidding: they imply to visitors that someone else owns the holy building and that it is not theirs.

This mention of holiness introduces us to another group who feel that they have a stake in cathedrals – the pilgrims. Among these are people with strong commitment and firm views as well as those whose views are less firm and whose faith is not easily articulated. Yet in their hearts they know that this is a place of holiness, where down the centuries prayer has been offered. They are seekers and believe that they too have a share in the place.

A related group includes those who drop into cathedral services. Some will come regularly. Others, with an equal but different religious perception, come less habitually but with no less seriousness. They seek to discover something of the relationship between themselves and the transcendent. Philip Toynbee describes them in his reflections on Evensong at Peterborough Cathedral. Arriving late he sits in the nave at a distance from the proceedings in the choir. He comments on the 'take it or leave it' nature of the ceremony and then continues: 'And yet we had not been only spectators of that deft performance; so far as each of us had found it possible we had also been participants. And if we had arrived five minutes earlier we would certainly have accepted the invitation to take two of those vacant places in the choir stalls.'[1] Part of Toynbee's experience that evening was to find space in a vast building for his own specific needs. It was a parable: at a distance from the focus of worship, he could still make the cathedral his own. The place belonged to him as much as it did to choir, canons and worshippers.

Owning the Church

Cathedrals are a fascinating subject for study in a discussion of 'ownership' of the church. In and around them, perhaps more than in any other aspect of church life, many different groups of people overlap. For example, Portsmouth Cathedral in a naval city finds itself the centre of certain expectations. From admirals to ratings the sailors look to it for something; for the rating it may be the right to be married there, a right belonging to anyone regularly sailing out of the port. By claiming this right the sailor articulates many things which are inexpressible about belonging to a city, a nation, the Navy, and so on. The list is probably endless. The admiral, by contrast, may regard it as the focus for all that he believes about the established church. He thinks of the cathedral as representing something transcendent about the order of the world to which he contributes through his leadership of the Navy. In Durham the chapel of The Durham Light Infantry will be an offence to some visitors and the focus of profound gratitude for others. Laid up military flags in every cathedral create the same dilemma.

And so we are brought to yet other groups of people who feel that they have a stake in the life of the church through their contact with a cathedral. The judges of the south-western circuit, for instance, will possibly feel that they have a stake in Exeter and Truro, where they attend the annual legal service. For the city fathers of Manchester or Leicester the cathedral may be their civic church. Many other organizations, academic or business, which often appear highly secular, will believe themselves to have a stake. At some point (perhaps to their surprise) they find themselves using 'their' cathedral.

Then there are those who are directly linked to the church and who will claim rites as well as rights. Most cathedrals have regular worshipping congregations, which in many cases are now organized into 'congregational councils'. Particularly in the newer cathedrals, which remain parish churches, the demands of tourists, of the secular world and even of pilgrims appear to be usurping the rights of the 'real' owners. Why should these people be allowed to dictate the arrangements in 'our cathedral'? And where does the diocese fit in? Ordinations, confirmations and youth celebrations can interrupt the weekly pattern of worship. A cathedral is the setting of the bishop's *cathedra*, the mother church of the diocese. Here is the place from which the bishop symbolically has exercised his pastoral and teaching role. People in the diocese may regard it as theirs and resent the competition of other groups.

The question of the identity of the church – its 'ownership' – is not an intellectual exercise; it touches upon matters of the heart and upon traditions, rites (and rights) which go back over many centuries and which probably can never be totally catalogued.

Common Ground

What is going on here? Cathedrals are a specific and accessible example of 'common ground', an idea with many resonances of common land and common rights intended for a variety of different groups. Cathedrals are large. Their size may mean that they attract hatred as symbols of power or of extravagance. Yet most people view them with affection and have no wish to see them crumble. Their size means not only that cathedrals stand out as potent symbols but also that they convey a message about the value of space. By contrast with the fragmentation which many increasingly experience, here is unity. It is a unity which can include those on the margins and is large enough to cope with issues (for example the tragedy of major disasters) for which other contexts may be too small. This role is best symbolized when the space is empty of obstruction – a cathedral nave empty of chairs and therefore 'useless' for mundane and immediate purposes is accessible. In an age when space is increasingly owned and belongs to individuals, here is common ground.

Cathedrals, and indeed many churches, are the places where any may enter and receive sustenance according to his or her need. Between the wars Dick Sheppard famously had this vision for St Martin-in-the-Fields:

> I stood on the west steps, and saw what this church could be to the life of the people. There passed by me into its warm inside, hundreds and hundreds of all sorts of people, going up to the temple of their Lord, with all their difficulties, trials and sorrows . . . And I said to them as they passed: 'Where are you going?' And they said only one thing: 'This is our home'.[2]

Of course, this passage is incurably sentimental. Many people treat church buildings just like any other tourist site and most do not come at all. Yet here is a picture of the power of awesome holiness and public common ground, which together compose the temple of the Lord.

The image of common ground clarifies the question of the identity of the church. What is held as a common becomes disputed territory, since so many groups see themselves as having a stake in it. A cathedral focuses the question through the building itself. In rural communities, though usually to a lesser extent in urban areas, the same is true of a parish church. Here, however, the picture is more complex. In the parish, as we have seen in earlier chapters, the identity of the church and its ownership is influenced by the minister, the representative person. His or her attitude toward the use of the building, toward the wider community and toward events such as baptisms and weddings, will determine people's perception of the church's identity and even the nature of God himself. Building and minister together speak of who, not what, the church is.

The community, however, builds its expectations of the church on a wider and more complicated front. This is difficult to grasp clearly, but evidence emerges in different ways. These wider expectations become prominent when we concentrate on the church's leadership at the national level. We noted above how the profile of the Archbishop of Canterbury has been heightened in recent years. National and international issues, disasters and thanksgivings, call for comment or ministration by the Archbishop. To a lesser extent the same is true of diocesan bishops. Hensley Henson's political attitudes made difficult his relations with working class people in the diocese of Durham and on one occasion almost endangered his life. David Jenkins, one of Henson's successors, is received more warmly in mining communities, whereas reactions have been more critical at a national level. On this wider canvas the focus shifts from buildings to an enlarged sense of representative people. These are not so much in themselves the leaders of the church as symbols of it.

There is, however, another and obvious side which we cannot ignore. Churches, not least cathedrals, attract many of the casualties of society who are lost for a home. Here they may feel safe and accepted. This is not simply because they are on neutral territory or even common ground. They may long for more. Sheppard again somewhat romantically saw this: 'Those same people would go on to say: "This is our home. This is where we are going to learn of the love of Jesus Christ. This is the altar of the Lord where all our peace lies. This is St. Martin's." It was reverent and full of love and they never pushed me behind a pillar because I was poor.'[3] Kenneth Riches, Bishop of Lincoln, called the cathedral 'a working space for the gospel' and it was Dean Bennett's ambition at Chester to make the place 'a great central, family house of God' where all would find a welcome. On this ground people would meet and experience something of the transcendent love of God.

Cumulatively these claims begin to sound too grand. It is all too easy for the church to pretend that it is at the centre of everyone's profoundest desires, which would be unleashed if only the right meeting place were provided or the right formula found. This is an error, for example, in some of the work done on 'implicit religion': people who do not see themselves as, in any sense, 'religious' are claimed as such. The concept of 'anonymous Christians' suffers from the same weakness. Society has in fact become secular in many respects. Proper questioning of the secularization thesis, especially when this is presented in a simplistic fashion, cannot dispose of this actuality. Realism is essential for anyone making claims for the church. It is indeed reasonable to ask at what point of numerical decline in public commitment to the church it would become unrealistic to claim that the church still has the cathedral-like task of providing common ground and try to work on that basis.

This point has not been reached. The way in which the common ground of cathedrals, parish churches and representative ministers continues to be used, and the more negative experience of groups fighting over the church's identity and who owns it, suggest that something of importance is still happening. Here groups meet in a way in which they do not appear to meet elsewhere.

Accessible Space: Transcendent Love

Seen in all their variety cathedrals can help us to a clearer understanding of the church. It is called to be an accessible space which speaks of God's transcendent love. This conclusion is not reached through a process of deduction from theological first principles: it arises from reflection on the evidence of people's behaviour. The buildings, the people (whatever their role) and the various activities and expectations speak of a church which wields considerable symbolic power for a wider community than its membership. If we ignore the power of these symbols, we may begin to believe that the Church of England can be self-sufficient and reorganize itself internally without reference to wider society. That way is not only a technical error: it also involves an unchristian exclusion of those who may be spiritually deprived.

Those with a stake in the church exist far beyond its confines as measured by any official method. It embraces more than regular communicants, more than the electoral rolls of parishes and more than those who attend services. When such people are allowed to feel that their claim on the church, however tenuous and tentative, is affirmed, the church can begin to exercise its role of prophecy and challenge within the wider society. If a spectrum of people in a society do not first sense that they are regarded as associated with the church and appreciate that it has some grasp of the issues which occur in their lives, any challenge from the church will be perceived as a reprimand or lecture. Prophecy on moral issues is expected of the church, even if it is not always welcomed. When it becomes political it is often rejected, although nevertheless an essential part of the gospel. Whatever the case no prophecy and challenge will be taken seriously if the church has not first proved itself accessible and empathetic, a common ground on which different groups may meet in order to seek the truth.

What model of the church does this discussion suggest? Many models have been employed at different times from the New Testament concepts, such as 'body of Christ' and 'new Israel', to theological ideas such as 'the church as an extension of the incarnation'. Avery Dulles has identified five classic models: the church as an institution, a mystical communion, a sacrament, a herald or a servant. Each of these, he argued, even the most unpromising of them, contained important truths about the church. None was exhaustive; they should be used to supplement and criticize each other.[4]

Each model also has something to say on the question of the identity and ownership of the church. Institutional models are clear about membership but less clear on ownership. We have, however, already stated reservations about the adequacy of this view in relation to the Church of England: membership is difficult to define with any certainty and criteria are necessarily absent. Mystical communion reminds us of the transcendent and godward nature of the church; it tells us that whoever else it may appear to belong to, the church ultimately belongs to God. Organizationally, however, it overarches thinking and has no immediate substance. Sacramental models draw attention to the symbolic power of buildings and of people in their roles. The herald church challenges and prophesies, but only when it possesses assigned authority to do so. Finally, the servant church shows the love of God, especially to those in need, and by making itself accessible to the world in which it is set.

To this outline, however, we should add the two ideas which derive from the experience of cathedrals and parish churches: 'common ground' and 'working space for the gospel'. These point to the accessibility of the church and its desirably disputed ownership. Nobody can trespass on common ground, since all may graze in a space which points to God and is protected by him. The role of the church's ministry is to tend the space and encourage people to venture into it and there encounter God's transcendent love.

To illuminate this approach to understanding the church, many images will be necessary. Such a variety of metaphors reflects theological vitality rather than contradiction. 'Common ground' has value as an image. But it may imply that nobody tills the ground or is responsible for it. Such a lack of control may enable all kinds of plants and animals to flourish on a common; it may also smack of anarchy. So the more we wish to employ it, the more a complementary, or balancing, image is needed. For this we propose the ancient biblical one which we have already mentioned: the church as the temple of the Lord. The temple had several courts and much of it was open to all. It was common ground on which all could meet: the Court of the Gentiles or Court of All Nations. At the heart of the temple, however, stood the Holy of Holies. Thus the temple was not a neutral place, for it always pointed to God. Furthermore it was never unattended, since it was the priests' task to enable people to be met by God.

'Cathedral', 'temple' and 'common ground' can supplement each other and assist us in identifying that amorphous idea which is fulfilling peoples' need for a space in which there can be meeting. Every spatial image allows a variety of groups with different and sometimes conflicting interests to encounter each other and to confront God. Each group wittingly or unwittingly has a stake in the church. The public ministers enable that church to be open in this way because it is coherently Christian, ever pointing to God who is its true owner.

Notes

1. Philip Toynbee, *Part of a Journey* (Collins, London, 1981), p. 198.
2. R. E. Roberts, *H. R. L. Sheppard* (Murray, London, 1942), pp. 91–2.
3. Roberts, *Sheppard*, pp. 91–2.
4. Avery Dulles, *Models of the Church*. Dublin, Gill & Macmillan, 1974.

7

ALTERNATIVE IMAGES

*The emphasis on a parochially based attitude for the
continuing ministry of the Church of England might seem
to take insufficient account of social changes. In this chapter
one of these changes, a major contributor to contemporary
society – the mass media – is discussed. From the perspective of the church's organization for ministry these media
can be seen as one means whereby the 'national parish' –
that network of gossip which is larger than anything local
but which is nevertheless experienced by people – is
sustained. The basic stance presented in this book remains
significantly true for something as new and apparently
foreign to the church as the mass media. For the parochial
model also offers an interpretation of the church's relationship to this new dimension to living. The thinking has been
informed by Angela Tilby.*

So far the running argument of this book has been that the
Church of England has a particular responsibility for what we
may call 'the soul of the nation'. Though all Christian churches
and other religious groups offer 'transcendental services', the
Church of England has this function uniquely assigned from
tradition and has believed it to be its distinctive vocation. Through
its establishment, and especially its parochial organization, it is
within reach of everyone. This 'reach' has a hierarchical structure
which mirrors those that are familiar in other aspects of English
life. We should not expect it to be otherwise. The Church of
England is a visible, public church which interlocks with English
life at various levels.

Local Gossip: Vicars and Bishops

Images of the Church of England and stories about its sayings and doings are mediated through society by gossip, print and the mass media – radio and television. These images and stories arise through an interaction between the messages which come from bits of the church – bishops, parsons, synods, societies – and what these provoke in readers, writers and broadcasters. In any communication there is a fundamental and inevitable tension between the message transmitted and the message received. The church is not immune from such strain.

These tensions are exacerbated by the dramatic success in the last sixty years of the mass media in creating a common arena for society's stories, images and messages. How far does the church survive as a visible institution in the new media? And how far should it expect to control the images and stories about it which the media purvey? In particular, how might the church conceptualize the relationship?

Images and stories about the church begin at the parish level. This, as we have noted, is the critical place of ministry and engagement with people in their homes and work. The church is visible as a building. It marks the landscape. It also has an inner life. There people pray and worship. A church building that has been closed or converted to another use, however striking its architecture, does not carry the same charge as one in which worship still takes place, however ordinary this may be. One pillar of our argument is that the priest and the church together still mark something for the communities in which they are set. The personal strengths or weaknesses of the vicar are less important than his ability to 'stand for' the church, for people in their various needs, for institutions, and through all this for God. The priest is, therefore, always facing two ways: towards the congregation and church and towards the context in which that church witnesses to God.

At the parish level images and stories are mediated to the congregation and to the community. This occurs within the church through sermons and teaching and to its environment by magazines, posters and notices. These comprise the conscious and deliberate messages which the church tries to send to the wider community. But concern with these may obliterate a more important organ of mediation and one over which the church has no control – gossip. Gossip comes from the congregation about the priest; it also arises within the wider community about the church. It percolates mysteriously. Sometimes it is benign, sometimes adulatory, sometimes speculative and sometimes malicious. Through gossip, however, a series of public images is built up about the priest and the church.

Church gossip is absorbing and informative. It can also be a source of anxiety and guilt for the priest. It is, however, inevitable. Christianity has given gossip a bad press. It can be destructive, but need not be. Human beings gossip and seem to need to do so. It creates fascinating images and transmits stories in a way that arouses interest. It is the core of the collection of shared narratives through which we construct meaning. Some of these stories get into the local newspapers. Stories become news, making the priest a local personality, a person with an image which is not all of his own creation. Such a person is the modern 'parson', an admixture of person and role which can be used by others to locate themselves in the world of meaning.

Gossip is the first and most primitive form of public media. It is important for the parish church because through it images and stories are spread far beyond the boundaries of the congregation to those for whom the church still speaks, positively or negatively, of some order that derives from the roots of history. This order carries memories of transcendence, moral purpose and the possibility of belonging, which sustain hope.

At a diocesan level the pattern continues. The church building is the cathedral and the parson is the bishop. In an earlier chapter the cathedral was described as offering a common space, which conveys something about God to worshippers and visitors alike. Its own image is partly constructed from what it produces by way of appeals, concerts, notices and so on, and partly by its image in the community, an image which is built up through gossip. This is always focused on personalities. So the image of the cathedral is closely woven into its history, to its ghosts as well as to its present endeavours.

The bishop may be regarded as a father in God to churchgoers, but at the level of city and country he is a personality. Gossip percolates about the bishop, often through the parish clergy. But his sayings and doings are reflected more formally at the level of local and national journalism and local radio. Several bishops are competent local radio presenters. Many of them have press officers to manage relationships with the media. And, like their clergy, they look in two directions. They face inwardly to the church at the endless round of confirmations and parish visits, as well as to the secret sufferings and ambiguities of those priests who confide in them. Outwardly bishops are expected to speak and act for the church, not as private individuals but as representative figures. Yet, as with the parish priest, the bishop is most liked when he personalizes the role.

National Gossip: The Archbishop of Canterbury

At another level, however, the Church of England is a national church. The persona who stands for the church in its national role is the Archbishop of Canterbury. He crowns the monarch, is second in order of precedence to the royal family and embodies the complications of the national role of the Church of England. However much an individual archbishop may set out to preach the gospel to an unconverted nation, or look to the unity of the churches under a reformed papacy, or see himself as first among equals in the Anglican communion, his primary role as far as the general public is concerned is to stand for the national church in a way that no other leader is allowed or expected to do. This image of this person is mediated through the mass media. Like the monarch he takes his place as part of the national continuing 'soap opera', which is another way of describing gossip at the level of the national establishment.

One effect of the mass media is to make the idea of the nation seem smaller and the gossip therefore more intimate. Its institutions become more sharply defined and its leaders more vulnerable to caricature. Everything, for instance, that the Archbishop of Canterbury says is grist to the mass media's mill and may be selected, quoted and used in evidence as part of the persisting saga of the church and nation.

The mass media look to the archbishop as a source of judgement or moral and spiritual authority on issues. That stance

75

does not necessarily mean that there is a public expectation that his proposals will work or even be acceptable. But he is expected to be clear, firm, kind and a little old-fashioned. The archbishop is there to remind the public that we were once a Christian nation. If this curious and vague expectation is not felt to be fulfilled, disappointment and even outrage ensue. Like the vicar and the diocesan bishop, the archbishop also has to cultivate the art of looking in two directions. Within the church he has diplomatically to handle its factions. The public, however, has a quite different, more diffuse and certainly less managerial expectation of him.

This two-facedness of the Church of England is both a weakness and a strength. The weakness is that the church does not possess the clarities of a sect, the available intimacy of the gathered body which is certain of the boundaries between it and the world. The Church of England is more an association of those who sense that the church belongs to them, whether or not they choose to do anything about it. Such a church is used by its public; it cannot dominate them or manipulate them. It is not necessarily powerful, although it may have considerable authority. The strength of such a position is that the Church of England has access to what is going on in an extraordinary way that is disproportionate to its actual size. It accompanies lives at many levels. At the same time its doings and sayings are gossip. They are the stuff of journalism, radio and television. If the mould that is described in this book is accurately perceived, then the church should recognize that it is there to be used by the mass media, just as it is by other publics at other levels.

Gossip, Church and Media

Today the common arena for what is gossiped about, for what is public and visible at all levels in society, is the media. This place might once have been the market place or the pub or any other focal institution within the parish, that area within which most of life is lived. Gossip is media. The mass media, then, represent the new 'parish', the area of life within which gossip has its place. Journalism and local radio are one level of media. Television is mass media with great reach and probably power. But it represents first and foremost the translation of gossip into images which are less argued about than absorbed.

It is hard for the church to understand television. It works on a different and unfamiliar scale from that of the parish, diocese or even nation. Church people are taught to work in places and with people, using words to open and develop relationships on a small scale. Their ministry is in every sense parochial, as is their theology. They simply do not have a theology which could take account of television. They do not understand how any medium could attempt to address millions. The expectations that they form about television are based on parochial experience and are often false when applied in a wider context. When television fails to deliver what they think it should, their criticism becomes bitter and derisory.

Yet television is changing us all the time. Its world is not simply a world of choice. Watching television is not like choosing to read a particular newspaper. Television is not one more channel of information among many: it is itself a milieu, more like literacy itself. Print was the technology that enabled literacy to spread through society instead of being the treasure of the few. It soon became clear that literacy was more than an effective way of passing on information. It coincided with and helped to bring about an expansion of knowledge and education. It gave ordinary people confidence to make judgements about their lives. It aided the process of secularization. It enabled people to envision new ways of being and, in the process, it sowed seeds of discontent and envy.

The long-term effects of universal 'tele-literacy' are impossible to judge. Television is still very young and is in the process of becoming. What we do see, however, is that it arouses the same excitement and anxiety, awareness and discontent as did the advent of literacy, but at a rate which we do not know how to assimilate. War, injustice, crime, famine, the destruction of the environment – history is being made which is instantly documented in vivid and memorable images. When the talk, analysis and opinion have been forgotten, the images remain as unforgettable marks on our consciences and consciousness: the Vietnamese prisoner being shot in the head, the victims of the Ethiopian famine, the lone student holding up the tank in Tiananmen

Square, the massed ranks of flowers and scarves at Hillsborough.

Some actively try to shape this new world of images; most participate passively and privately. It mirrors us, our attitudes and behaviours, yet in a way that separates us from the context of our lives. In this place we are susceptible both to the cries and griefs of the world, and also to the tremendous excitement of worldly success and achievement. Victims, villains and heroes are all present.

When television mediates the church, it does so on the same grand scale. It looks for the big story, for the leaders and heroes and victims. It hunts the great quarrels and dramatic reconciliations. Like gossip, the media exalt individuals and pulls them down to size. This is why they expect the Archbishop of Canterbury to be a leader and delight to find fault with him. It is also why they treat the church with sceptical distance and sometimes amusement. But it is also why they are interested in the church's conflicts, whether these are over doctrine, politics or sex.

The Church and Alternative Images

Christianity possesses a well-developed critique of gossip. It is allied to lying and slander and condemned as idle. Behind such criticisms lies the fear that gossip has power to mediate stories and images which are beyond the control of the appointed authorities. Mass media have the same power as gossip, only on a much larger scale. They are the environment in which our common stories are now held and shared, our conflicts and misunderstandings are expressed, our fears and hates given names and faces. We might say, therefore, that they make more conceivable the idea of a 'national parish', that is, a new zone of human experience which extends far beyond experienced community to believed or felt community. Alongside local culture there is now a new national culture and the interplay between them is as yet unclear.

The attitude of the church to the media, therefore, is not just that of an interested party to a debate. There is a common interest and consequently implicit competition. Some, mostly evangelicals, argue that the church should take a stronger grip on the mass media. They are methodical about mastering the arts of graphic design, story writing, photography and public relations. They believe that slickness is the key and that if the product is professional it will win air-time. They also tend to surmise that the media can be taught, controlled and sometimes even bought. There was a memorable encounter between a salesman for Jimmy Swaggart's programmes and John Whale of the BBC, which was marked by mutual incomprehension. For the one any TV station was like any other and the status of the BBC was beyond him; for the other it seemed unbelievable that the salesman was so ignorant and hence that there must be a hidden dimension to the transaction. The 'televangelists' buy time and produce slick worship. There are Christian groups in the UK which are racing to win time on new European networks.

Some clergy explicitly see themselves and their activity as being in competition with television. They devise various strategies for coping with their dilemma. One, for example, takes a video of himself talking about baptism on his baptism visits. On arrival he slots it smartly into the video recorder, thus thinking to give himself the authority of what comes out of the television and so pre-empting all other signals. The assumption is that in a world saturated by television the answer is to add to the babble by making sure that the high clear voice of the gospel is as loud as, or even louder than, any of the competing voices.

But all such strategies are attempts at control and underlying their deployment is a struggle involving more than the churches. But because the Church of England is caught up so intimately with British culture, it is inevitable that it should especially feel this struggle and find the battle also being waged within itself. There are those who look to the American model of a free-market economy in religion and hope for a matching market in the media. This approach is unlikely to succeed, since such a market of religious choice is not part of the basic culture in the United Kingdom. In addition, it takes insufficient account of the parochial (in the sense in which we have been using this term) dimension of the Church of England. The 'market' in people's minds is not as open as some assume. Amid the uncertainty about the media, however, the church is also recipient of that expectation which is familiar to it in all aspects of its life, namely

79

that it will stand for some sort of integrity in the face of the change. In this instance the changes are those being brought about by the Broadcasting Bill, especially with regard to religious advertising.

People who invest in strategies of control display a mentality which understands Christianity only in terms of a struggle for power. Yet such an approach is itself corrupting, as is clear from the tragi-comedy of American televangelism. The investment of the Protestant pastors in commercial television has had enigmatic effects on the gospel that they preach. Televangelism has led to a softening of traditional evangelical theology, a lack of prophetic edge, an easy acceptance of the products of materialism and an alliance of Christianity with the American dream. The outcome is the risk of being overwhelmed by financial and sexual temptation. Those Christian leaders who play the media like film stars may find themselves living out the worst fate of their models.

The reverse side of this coin is a puritanism which sees mass media as essentially corrupting and trivial. This attitude belongs less to the Protestant world than to a variety of lobbies within the churches. There is a left-wing anti-consumerist lobby which rejects television for its supposed elevation of passive pleasure and material goods. There is also a more right-wing and theologically conservative lobby which rejects television on the grounds that it destroys family life and encourages illicit sex and violence. So the message comes from both groups, often bearing the label 'Christian', that television is a dangerous and controlling force, which quells dissent and encourages passivity, individualism and greed. At best it wastes time which could be better spent working, praying, learning, caring or building up family relationships.

A more subtle critique suggests that television encourages casual scepticism which is inimical to the gospel. It contributes so much to our saturation with images that it prevents us from taking anything with complete seriousness. Religion is treated with a weary 'seen-it-all-before' agnosticism which assaults the possibility of living faith. There is some substance in this judgement. Television does assume a liberal, if fairly tolerant, scepticism in its audience. It does pitch itself in a tone which is critical of authority, while sometimes being uncritical of its own power and influence. Church critics have charged religious broadcasters with selling out to scepticism instead of producing challenging apologetic programmes which present the possibility of belief in God and the claims of Jesus Christ.

It is possible to sympathize with the frustration behind these attacks. But they are misplaced. The scepticism which television exudes may be enhanced by the nature of the medium, but it is rooted in an attitude which all have inhabited since the First World War. This is not an age of public, visible and commonly-held faith. Agnosticism is the spirit of the age, combined with a private and rather wooden belief in God, which generally has nothing directly to do with the church. There may be hunger for a richer faith, but if so the churches have so far failed to identify and respond to this. There is a limited extent to which television can fill the gap. This medium can only articulate and express such longing for faith as there might be and the memory of what once was. In view of this, the churches might derive encouragement from the amount of religious material that appears in the mass media. Like the attendance of 'fringe' people in the parishes, this represents a continuing religious life which the Church of England should not and for its own future dare not ignore.

The Particular Role of the Church of England

The Church of England does not have to choose between joining the struggle for control or totally rejecting the media. It sometimes falls for this dichotomy because it fails to locate the media in terms which makes them part of the church's world. Rather than being conceived as something structurally beyond the church's comprehension, the modern mass media are better thought of in terms of an alternative, national 'parish'. Obviously they are not in any sense the church's congregation. But they are like those whose faith is occasionally evidenced but whose lives are not directly linked with the church. But if this is so, one of the most urgent challenges facing the church is the creation of a theology of the media.

A church which has inherited and seeks to sustain close connections with the identity of the nation has to be competent in its dealings with the mass media, which link together all those facets of social life which make up 'the national parish'. Television lives, exactly as does the church, by a series of interactions. The two are also joined through a concern for communication. This is the heart of the gospel. The ability to communicate is expressed and reaffirmed in every liturgical act. Communication involves dialogue. And there is a prophetic and priestly dimension. With this few would argue. Yet it is usually overlooked that all media work at this juncture parallels the life of the church, because it has to do with the transmission of words and images, which is a sacred task. Not in vain is prayer offered for those who 'speak where many listen and write what many read'. And, like the church, the media are especially excoriated when they fail to conform to popular expectations.

Like the church, too, the media must remain interactive, if they are not to lose their vocation and credibility. The mass media of Eastern Europe, for example, were controlled by the authorities in such a way that, although there were large audiences for the radio and television, the output was not believed. They had ceased to mediate, because one-way control is not mediation (itself a Christian theme) but dictation which produces dictatorship. By contrast, so it seems, the churches, although not well attended, nevertheless on the whole retained their credibility as places of interaction between people, and so as the protests began people were able to make some greater use of them.

The British mass media are far from perfect. The images that they mediate of the Church of England are varied in quality and accuracy. There is a good deal of ignorance and prejudice about the church, its beliefs, doctrines and forms of ministry. This is faithfully reflected by the mass media and should be usefully informative to the church. Much could be put right by attention to the media, by learning their crafts, not in order to control or to perform well, but to influence the building up of more reliable images of what the church is and what it stands for. Just as at the parochial and diocesan level the gossip is only affected in so far as the church participates, so at the level of the national parish sustained by the mass media, the message will become more faithful only if the church participates and does not seek merely to use the media.

The large scale, but still parochial style, of interaction which the media make possible, can be seen in those moments when television presents the Church of England as it is and as it is perhaps perceived by the majority of people in this country. These are the occasions of national celebration or mourning. Such events lie beyond the church's control, but are also instances when the church may be shown in its best and truest light. National celebrations are rare. The next will probably be a coronation. Most lesser celebrations exclude or offend one or more sections of society. But disasters numb all and, what is more, seem to be frequent. These reveal the Church of England as a pastoral non-judgemental church, whose ministry is genuinely open to all. It is deeply interlocked with the suffering and healing of ordinary people at all levels of society.

At such times television is always present. It descends where there is strife and disaster, to some extend adding to the disarray. In such circumstances the local vicar is often the person who is invited to articulate the grief or heroism of the people. For a moment his is a trusted and significant voice. Because he is provided to be and to pray there, when the cameras come he is the person whom they find. Even in Northern Ireland the media turn to the priest on the spot in the community, whether he be Roman Catholic or Protestant, to utter the repetitious but needed words. In any other context such reiteration would turn the media off; here they gossip for the nation and use the local minister to mouth the inevitably inadequate but needed words. In England this role almost always falls to the Church of England vicar or bishop, or sometimes to the archbishop.

The message of the media seems still to be that the Church of England has a future as an institution that touches deeply some of the most sensitive areas of national life. This ministry, for that is what it is, is recognized and reflected by the mass media, even when the church itself may minimize its importance. Even the mockery is rarely very hostile. For the church, without some attention to the significance of the media, the notion of 'national' in its thinking will decline. For the media are now the main articulators of life on this scale. They consistently remind the church of its 'alternative parish', that undefined national expectation that often finds expression through moments on the media. The church's parochial mentality, provided it can take account of these alternatives and remain sufficiently large, provides a continuing model for discerning that engagement and its contemporary manifestations. This may not be the role that some within the church would like or an interaction which they would desire. But both are dimensions of human life with which any national church should feel at home.

8

BISHOPS AND SYNODS

Ideas about the church and ministry abound. But the practicalities of church life are such that any approach to these issues must not only be theologically grounded and based in the realities of people's experience and behaviour; it must also be capable of being embodied in church structures. It has been a general problem in the contemporary church that structural thinking has tended to be insulated from the human realities of the church and ministry. In this chapter some of the difficulties which the Church of England has created for itself are explored and adjustments proposed. The thinking is primarily informed by Paul Bates and Tim Stevens.

There is 'confusion and competition as to who is in charge of the Church: the House of Bishops or the Standing Committee of [General] Synod'. So said Mark Santer, Bishop of Birmingham, in his address to his diocesan synod on 26 June 1990. His words, echoed by other bishops in similar addresses, are what someone has described as 'the tip of an episcopal iceberg of discontent' about the General Synod of the Church of England.

There are other complaints: 'Few ordinary church members feel themselves to have a stake in its [the General Synod's] deliberations, and only a small number of the clergy take an interest.'[1] The criticism is not new. The Report on Church and State in 1970 included the comment that, 'As long as the General Synod meets during the week, it will be dominated by the retired, the leisured and the professional classes'. This has usually been taken to refer to the laity who are free to stand for election to the synod. But it may, of course, be as true of the clergy.

The Synod as a Problem

These quotations were taken from a number of articles which were published in a church newspaper around the time of the meeting of General Synod at York in July 1990. They may have been evidence of an unrepresentative campaign to alter the balance of power in the Church of England. There are, after all, controversial decisions to be made during the lifetime of the Synod in the 1990s. It may be that what was heard was nothing but the ritual parading of combatants. The battles between the various factions within the Synod have been heated, as have attitudes to the bishops. To quote the Bishop of Birmingham again:

> Mistrust and downright hostility towards the episcopate and the Archbishop of Canterbury in particular is most evident at Question Time. No Church can be healthy whose elected representatives show so little respect towards the office of their chief pastor. The institutionalisation of mistrust is evident in every piece of synodical legislation which further restricts the power of bishops to exercise their pastoral office freely.

That could be interpreted as a cry of anguish from a representative of a powerful group whose power was being wrested from it. But the theme, albeit expressed in different words, occurs in many quarters and is implicitly addressed in the preparatory document to the forthcoming review of the working of the synodical system. These remarks, therefore, indicate the difficulty that the Church of England has in deciding what it may be to be a synodically governed episcopal church, and suggest that it is becoming more aware that there is a genuine problem. The issue is not just one of organization; it touches the church at its theological heart.

The Episcopal Slipstream

The issue can be illustrated by an example that originates elsewhere than in the General Synod. At a conference for diocesan officers for Continuing Ministerial Education (CME), a workshop was held on the relationship between the bishop and

the CME officer in the diocese. Nearly a third of the dioceses of
the Church of England were represented and, as the issues
involved were explored, a fundamental division began to emerge.
Some officers worked almost exclusively through Councils or
Boards of Ministry in the diocese, acting as their executive
officer. They found that they spent nearly as much time trying to
persuade those Councils and Boards of the value of a piece of
work, particularly if it incurred costs, as they did in actually
doing it. The Boards and Councils were behaving correctly in
wanting to ensure proper accountability to diocesan synod. But
the officers found the process frustrating, even to the extent of
(in their view) nullifying their efforts to encourage CME.

By contrast other officers found themselves working much
more as an agent of the bishop. They spent time with him,
'tucked into his slipstream', as the workshop coined the phrase.
They also found that they had more opportunity to be creative
and innovative. They did not ignore the proper processes of the
synodical structure, but worked outside, or perhaps alongside,
them.

Which kind of CME officer any individual was allowed to be
depended on the bishop and the way he saw his role *vis-à-vis*
synod more than on the officer and certainly more than it did on
synod. During the reflection at the end of the workshop, people
commented that this was true of all diocesan officers. They
always experienced tension between being an officer of synod,
accountable to it for spending money and sensitive to it about the
work, and being a bishop's officer, sharing and in some way
exercising part of the bishop's oversight.

On the one hand, officers realise that they have a particular
responsibility to the Boards and Committees that they serve,
but, on the other hand, they feel that their priesthood is
somehow being devalued if there is no direct contact with the
bishop . . . They do not want to see themselves as mere
functionaries and servants of the committees, yet neither do
they wish to cut themselves off from the whole synodical
system that they are serving.[2]

Episcopal and Synodical Systems

The problem is familiar and one that is endemic to the contemporary church. It is felt so acutely that everyone feels that he or she has something to contribute to its solution, or at least to salving the hurts of those involved. But in such a welter of debate and amid such emotive topics, clarity is essential. One way of clarifying what is happening comes through distinguishing two distinct systems. The one is *episcopal*: within it authority derives from the bishop and the range of roles that he holds. The other is *synodical*, and its authority stems from the fact that through an election procedure the people of God, lay and ordained, are represented. Complications arise because individuals simultaneously occupy and exercise roles in each system, which can lead to an unhelpful blurring.

The diocesan bishop, for instance, 'leads' the diocese (generalized activity) and presides over the diocesan synod (a specific and limited role). We may compare his suffragan colleague, in whom often these confusions are even more strongly located. Sometimes in the absence of the diocesan, he specifically represents the bishop of the diocese; at other times, however, he may be assigned a role which does not derive in any way from his being the diocesan's deputy. For example, he may chair a diocesan Board of Ministry. This is a synodical body and his chairing of it will have nothing particular to do with his role as suffragan. Yet questions of ministry ultimately relate to the diocesan bishop. The Board may seek to avoid some decisions and try to escape referring them actually to the diocesan bishop by implicitly inviting the suffragan to deal with them, neither in his role as chairman nor in his role as deputy to the diocesan bishop. Unless he is very clear, the chances are that the suffragan will act in his own perceived role as 'a bishop', thus finding himself unclear about which authority he should invoke and, what is more, encouraging unclarity in others.

We might draw an analogy in parliamentary terms: it is as though the Prime Minister was also the Speaker of the House of Commons, or the Foreign Secretary also the Chairman of the Select Committee on Foreign Affairs. The degree of sophistication required to sort out the roles in such hypothetical

88

situations is some indication of the degree of sophistication required from those involved in the episcopal and synodical systems if there is not to be chaos. And even if those occupying these complex roles can discern their complicated authority, there is little chance that those among whom they work and minister will grasp the issues. What is more, in the church it is probable that leaders (not least the bishops) will have to assume a multitude of roles, some of which are overt (such as that of chairman) but some of which are almost covert (such as that of spiritual example). The way in which the difficulty is customarily avoided is by reference to the personality of the bishop or to the need for better personal relationships within the structures. Chaos may be overcome for a while by force of personality, but it is unlikely to become a long-term solution.

The potential muddle is found not only at a diocesan level. The same confusion occurs in the parishes. The parish priest leads worship in the church building and chairs the Parochial Church Council in the hall. A parishioner is a worshipper in the church building and a member of the PCC in the hall. It is sometimes hard for both not to carry appropriate behaviour in one area (that of worship) into the other (the PCC). The chair of the PCC is, for example, an inappropriate place from which to preach a sermon, often though it might happen. Some vicars seek to restrict the possible confusion of roles by inviting the vice-chairman to chair the meeting as often as possible. Church-wardens will express a similar shift from one system to another with phrases which begin, 'Wearing my churchwarden's hat, vicar . . .'

The Church of England's organizational problem, therefore, is not merely theoretical. At present it pervades its life and affects all its activities and intentions. This church has always been an *episcopal* church, believing that the bishop's oversight is essential. The bishop is the focal human symbol in the church: he, the local link with the church catholic, assigns authority to minister. This perception is traditionally expressed by the presence of the bishop's chair in the sanctuary of every church, so that in each parish church, as in the cathedral, the bishop's *cathedra*, his seat, is located. When the bishop institutes an incumbent, he entrusts him with the care of the spiritual well-being of the parish by handing over to him 'the cure of souls that is both thine and mine'. The more recent version is, 'Receive the pastoral care of this parish that is both yours and mine', which reflects a limited and inaccurate notion of 'cure'. 'Cure' is more powerful and frightening than 'care': it includes the idea of the minister's responsibility for the eternal destiny of the soul and the educational function of teaching what the soul needs to know for its health.

The bishop also lays hands on every ordained minister and says, 'Take thou authority' (weakened in the new Ordinal to 'Receive this book as a sign of the authority . . .'), that is, the authority belonging to the bishop by virtue of his office and exercised by being joined with the work of the parish priest. The latter is not there simply because he or she likes the area or because the congregation wants them. He or she, joined with the bishop, is able through that connection, which is both formal and felt, to represent the authority of the wider church.

The Synodical Addition

This simple and elegant system has had grafted onto it another system in which authority stems from another form of representation – election. It could be argued that the movement towards the modern synodical system was encouraged in the church because the bishops proved incapable of exercising the kind of authority spelled out in the last paragraph. Perhaps Trollope destroyed for ever the possibility of real *episcope* being exercised. The synodical idea, however, is not merely the product of a more democratic age. John Habgood, the Archbishop of York, explored this thought in a sermon delivered to the meeting of General Synod at York in 1990. He encouraged the congregation to 'take utterly seriously the synodical idea'.

There do seem to have been various groupings, large and small, which gave shape to the early church . . . Perhaps it is not so absurd to jump from [St Luke's account (Luke 10.1–20) of] the sending out of the seventy to the Synod. At least we can take the point that such ruling bodies are not a modern bureaucratic invention. The notion that within the whole people of God a defined number of people can bear responsibility has deep roots in our scriptural beginnings.

Bishops, clergy and laity meet to 'take counsel together in the name of Christ' on behalf of the whole Church.[3]

When the Synodical Government Measure of 1969 was drawn up, an attempt was made to hold together these two systems, the episcopal and the synodical. The functions of General Synod were, first to make provision in respect of matters concerning the Church of England by Measure, intended to be given the force and effect of an Act of Parliament, or by Canon, and second to consider and express their opinion on any other matters of religious or public interest. But 'a provision touching doctrinal formulae or the services or ceremonies of the Church of England or the administration of the Sacraments or sacred rites thereof shall . . . be referred to the House of Bishops.'[4] The bishops, however, are not the sole or final reference in such matters. The House of Clergy or the House of Laity can ask for a provision touching such matters to be submitted for approval to each House.

The functions of a diocesan synod were differently ordered by being the reverse of those assigned to General Synod. A diocesan synod was first to consider matters concerning the Church of England, to make provision for such matters in relation to the diocese and to consider and express opinions on any matters in relation to the diocese and to consider and express its opinion on any matters of religious or public interest. These tasks echo those of General Synod. Second the diocesan synod was to advise the bishop on any matters on which he may consult it. And third, it was to consider and express its opinion on any matter referred by General Synod. The Measure adds, 'It shall be the duty of the bishop to consult with diocesan synod on matters of general concern and importance to the diocese.'[5] Significantly, there is no direction in cases where the bishop and synod disagree on what constitutes a matter of general concern or significance to the diocese.

The full complexities of the Measure need not concern us here. They will probably be subject to scrutiny in the forthcoming review of the way in which the synods work. The relationships between the House of Bishops and General Synod, and between the diocesan bishop and the diocesan synod seem to be in principle clear and to provide a basis by which they might work together. At first sight there certainly does not seem to be cause for some of the anxiety expressed in the quotations at the beginning of this chapter. There must, therefore, be some underlying unclarity or conflict which has emerged in practice.

The Apostolic and Diaconal Systems

To discern what this might be, it may be helpful to use another way of describing the systems within the church. Bruce Reed has helpfully drawn a distinction between the two basic systems which operate in the church. He calls these 'the apostolic system' and 'the diaconal system'.[6] The former incorporates all the activities that are included in the primary task of the church as an institution, chiefly worship, preaching and pastoring. 'The diaconal system' comprises the activities that the institution requires to continue to function. Among these we may, for instance, discern the need for policy to be drawn up, both strategic and tactical. Once a church embarks on activities, it needs some servicing, which is also a function of the diaconal system, and a means of administering the resources available. All these are necessary if the apostolic work of the church is to be carried out.

When we look at the Church of England with this framework of thought, two things become obvious. The first is that the primary task of the church, what the church is for, is crucial. Not only does its definition determine the activities which belong to the apostolic system, it also clarifies what belongs to the diaconal system. The second is that according to the 1969 Measure both the bishop and the synod have functions within each system.

For example, in a parish the Parochial Church Council is concerned with both the apostolic and the diaconal systems. It obviously has many functions in sustaining the life of the local church. But it is also required to collaborate with the vicar in promoting the ministry and mission of the church in that place. The parish priest is the bishop's colleague in apostolic activity and co-chairman of the PCC. The experience of many PCCs is that the demands of the diaconal system frequently dominate. Drains, finance and fetes become preoccupations. In order to maintain concern for the ministry and mission of the church some PCCs have adopted the device of having a special agenda item at each meeting that is specifically focused on the work of the apostolic system. It does not come naturally, but has to be assigned specific attention. Another way of describing this phenomenon is to say that there is a pervasive tendency for facets of the diaconal system to become the primary task of the church. For example, it may be that the upkeep of the building becomes the primary task, or the financial viability of the church, or that education programmes, study and Bible study groups, become the most important feature in the life of the church.

The same issue emerges at the diocesan level. The bishop is crucially a leader in the apostolic system of the church's activity. Both he, the clergy and the people are constantly reminded of this when he institutes a new incumbent with the public affirmation of the responsibility for the well-being of the parish shared by the bishop and the parish priest. He also has a leadership role in the diaconal system as 'bishop in synod', which is practically expressed in diocesan boards or committees, and the work of any suffragan bishop, archdeacons, registrars, rural deans and diocesan advisers and officers.

There may be disagreement in all of this as to which system any particular committee or officer belongs to. That will be endemic in any organization, such as the church, which is a mix of voluntary and employed workers. The advantage of this suggested basic distinction is that, at any given moment, bishops, clergy or others with roles in the church have a framework for testing in which system they are operating, and therefore what are the limits of their authority and, more importantly, the genuine opportunities being presented.

Thus within the apostolic system, it will be proper for the bishop to exercise his episcopal authority by sending out a pastoral letter in which he reminds his clergy and the people of some aspect of the church's primary task. Such a procedure, however, would not be appropriate within the diaconal system. There, although the bishop is the nominal head, if he tries to make this actual by taking direct charge, he is likely to confuse the recipients of his message. How are they to know whether it comes from the head of the apostolic system and therefore may be presumed to have something to do with the church's essential activity and mission, or from the head of the diaconal system, and therefore have something to do with the church's maintenance task? And if these two systems are given equal authority, it will not be long before the easier (the diaconal) will replace the harder (the apostolic). So any message within the diaconal system will probably be delegated to an archdeacon or a secretary.

Uncertainty about the source of authority may be an underlying reason for the frustration which many feel with diocesan mailings, a large envelope full of various papers that arrives at regular intervals on a parish priest's desk. It may contain suggestions about where to buy oil, notice of a new study course, a message from the diocesan secretary about the car mileage allowance and a letter from the bishop about the Decade of Evangelism. The recipients do not know how to deal with such a mixture of messages. On the surface they all make sense. In terms of the working of the church they convey such confused messages about authority that they can only end up in the waste-paper bin.

Competition for Authority

The difficulties of a diocesan mailing may seem a long way from the problem of organizing an episcopal and synodical church. They have in common, however, a capacity to arouse irrational antipathy. Few, when asked, doubt the need for more communication and hence for mailings. Equally, few when questioned wish to abandon the advantages of synodical discussion and decision-making. In both cases, however, it is clear that tinkering with the superficial will make little difference, whether this be using coloured paper in a mailing or revising the standing orders of a synod. The fundamental issue to be addressed is that of authority, which in practical terms emerges in the difference between those who have authority and the capacity to act and to do things and those whose authority is to create the policy framework for such activity and ensure some resource is available.

The irate use of the waste-paper bin may be a further symptom of the discontent with the tendency of the diaconal system to push out the apostolic work. Diocesan officers, for example, wish to escape from the diaconal system of committees because it seems to prevent them from doing their real job, that of being a piece of the bishop in the apostolic system. At the level of diocesan or General Synod, the equivalent of drains, fetes and finance becomes a major preoccupation. So the agenda and conflict are about money and information. The real business, what the church is for, seems to disappear, even if talked about in demagogic appeal. It is not long before the bishop or bishops see themselves as sole guardians of the apostolic system, protecting it against the encroaching diaconal system of synodical boards and councils.

This again brings us to the primary task of the church. Clarity about this is essential if the distinction between the apostolic and diaconal systems is to be usefully sustained. The real basis for the confusion to which the Bishop of Birmingham refers lies here: the bishops and the synods do not share a common perception of the church's task. The bishops, because of their particular role on the boundary of the diocese and the rest of society, are aware of how they and the church relate to society. In their experience they sense and know about the Church of England's relation to society and hence about the primary task of the church. The parish system, the parish priest, establishment and even episcopacy, all point to a concern for society as a whole, however well or badly that concern is expressed. That is not to say that others may not be equally aware: it is to say that the bishops have a distinctive responsibility to be aware and function in the system to carry such awareness. This is interestingly demonstrated by what is often said to happen to those who are made bishop. However much before their consecration their understanding of the church was distant from this primary task, they soon seem to change their views. Some describe this as 'the removal of any back-bone'; others say that they know no one who has been improved by consecration. Yet in fact these changes are more likely to exemplify in the church's leaders the distinctive calling of the Church of England.

Almost in reaction, so it seems, the synodical system becomes preoccupied with the internal life and trying to hold the bishops and clergy control to an internally developed model of existence. So the diaconal system of management and service becomes for synods the primary task of the church. That may be why the synod fails to organize itself so that it is not dominated by 'the retired, the leisured and the professional classes' and why it continues to meet during the week. To become an expert in the diaconal system takes time and energy, both in attendance at meetings and in reading the papers and participating in extra-synodical activity, both formal and informal. It is significant how often in election addresses candidates emphasize their experience of the synodical system. Yet in terms of understanding the church's involvement with society and the different, but complementary, roles of clergy and laity in that mission, it might be considered more useful for potential candidates to be able to sustain contact with society and the church's function in it through their knowledge of and presence in the world of employment.

In this regard it may be worth noting that the most publicly significant engagements of the Church of England with society in recent years have been the result of episcopal initiative rather than synodical – the Falklands service, The Commission on Urban Priority Areas and that on Rural Areas. Indeed, the last of these was not even financed by Synod and the Report was not published by the Church Information Office.

Two Ideas of Representation

There may, however, be a further reason why the episcopal and synodical systems find themselves in competition. This has to do with the idea of representation. The argument of this book is that the Church of England acts in various ways 'on behalf of' others in society. Worshippers, for instance, assemble as representatives of a wider group. Non-worshippers may still feel that the church belongs to them. Such a feeling need not, of course, belong only to the worship of the Church of England. That claim would be merely arrogant. The contention is that it ought at least to belong to it. A small, apparently insignificant, number of people in church may in fact represent many hundreds. Without this belief a church will feel that it has to try and draw everyone into membership. The result is likely to be the proliferation of activities which belong to the diaconal system – the need to have enough members to be economically viable, or to be a significant presence in the community, or the predominance of events that will attract newcomers because of their social content – dominating those belonging to the apostolic function of the church.

Understood in this way, a bishop can represent a diocese and act on its behalf. When he acts, in a sense the whole diocese acts, representatively. In the same way, when the assembled bishops act, they do so on behalf of the whole church. One small, but significant indicator of this, is the way in which there is increasingly differentiation drawn between the House of Bishops (a synodical house, serviced by the secretariat) and the Bishops' Meeting (which is not bound by synodical procedure).

There is, however, a competing understanding of representation, which suggests that for a group of people to be truly representative of a wider whole, all the separate parts of that whole must be present. For example for General Synod to be truly representative, it must have a proper balance of Evangelicals, Catholics, Liberals, Radicals, and so on, as well as a balance between all the other differences of race, class, age, gender, geography and so on. Such a make-up must produce the predominant experience of fragmentation. A member's first loyalty will be to those who put him or her in Synod. Loyalty to the whole body will be secondary; that to the promoting group primary. In political terms, it is the difficulty that a member of parliament has in representing all the constituents, not merely those who voted for him or her. One way of fostering a loyalty to the whole is the emphasis that is given to the institution of Parliament. For members of General Synod (as indeed of the other synods) to put their allegiance to the whole above their allegiance to their party or particular passion, is to ask for a notion of representation which is at present contrary to that which put them there in the first place.

An instance of the problem and an indication of its seriousness may be seen in the issue of the ordination of women. It is proving very difficult to see how one gender can represent the other: a man cannot represent a woman, and *vice versa*: both must be present in order to ensure adequate representation, which is a version of the 'must-have-all-the-constituent-parts' idea. This

97

problem may be a passing phase, as society and the church struggle to right the injustices of centuries. It is theologically and pastorally important, however, for it to be seen to be and to become such an interlude. For unless one person can represent another, regardless of gender, race, class or geography, it will become hard to interpret the significance of the life and death of Jesus in any but the most crudely substitutionary terms. 'Instead of' is different from 'on behalf of'.

Not only, therefore, may bishops and synods have different perceptions of the church's task; they also understand representation in different ways. Both bishop and synod are 'ideas in the mind' – that is, only if people believe in the idea of 'bishop' and that he does things, whether they agree or not, on their behalf, can the bishop act with any authority in his diocese. Equally, the bishop must believe passionately in the office, if he is to work at what it means to do things on behalf of the whole church and so act with genuine authority and not be deluded into belief in his power. Similarly members of synods and those who elect them must believe in the idea of 'synod', that they meet on behalf of the whole and take counsel on behalf of the whole church.

It may be that today bishops find it harder to believe passionately in their office. There is certainly a tendency among both clergy and laity to be cynical about them. It seems genuinely hard for people to believe strongly in synods, whether General, diocesan or deanery. Yet without some prior belief in the importance and possibility of corporate representation, the relationship between bishops and synods becomes merely a power struggle over which has control of the other. A diocesan synod tends to employ finance as its weapon. General Synod resorts to courteous invective.

This discussion of what appears to be the basic organizational structure of the Church of England has raised many issues which touch the church at its theological heart. It leads directly to consideration of what the church is for – a question which is ultimately about God and how he relates to the world. It also invites examination of the nature of representation, which is ultimately about the nature of Christ. It also reopens the question of the clash between a monarchical and a democratic view of the church, in which sociological and historical issues slide into theological ones about the nature of the trinitarian God.

Notes

1. *The Church Times*, 29 June and 6 July 1990.
2. The Diocese of Lincoln, Board of Ministry.
3. John Habgood, Sermon in York Minster, 8 July 1990.
4. The Synodical Government Measure (1969), p. 4.
5. ibid., pp. 11–12.
6. *The Dynamics of Religion*. London, Darton, Longman and Todd, 1978.

9

CHURCH AND CULTURE

The Church of England cannot be conceived without reference to English culture. This connection is sometimes regarded only as a burden which should be shed as soon as possible. Certainly it puts demands on this particular church which are different from those experienced by some others, both in this country and elsewhere. Nevertheless, this church is embedded in a culture which it has served for a very long time. As a result it has become a major bearer of symbols for that culture. This situation is both given and an opportunity. The more constricted theological thinking about the church becomes, the more incomprehensible such a responsibility appears. The ideas here have been developed by Bernice Martin.

This book opened with the question, 'Is there a future for the Church of England?'. The subsequent affirmations have also been enquiries as to whether it is either realistic or proper to hope for an institutional future. By many of its most obvious criteria Christianity in general – and the Church of England in particular – might be diagnosed as in a more advanced state of entropy in Britain than anywhere else in the West, with the exception of Scandinavia. Regular religious practice and active institutional commitment have been at a low level for many decades in all the Protestant cultures of Northern Europe. The younger generations sit ever more loose to the religion of their forebears. The only points of growth seem to lie outside the mainstream in the charismatic and fundamentalist renewal movements. But even these make only a tiny bump in the graph of what appears to some an inexorable institutional decline. Yet in spite of this, the Church of England seems to continue to play

100

an indispensable role in the life of the nation, a role which should not be lightly abandoned.

The Flame of Faith

The church's witness is manifested in substantive ways in that network of relationships and activities that mark its life and ministry. The much quoted indices of institutional inertia are not the only ones by which to judge the significance of the church and, even more importantly, to prejudge its future role. Most people, after all, would have reckoned the churches in Eastern Europe (apart from those in Poland) impotent and even moribund, until they revealed themselves as reservoirs of latent meaning and the natural focus for communal action in the overthrow of state communism during the spring of 1990. Who, for example, considering the exiguous hold of Christianity in Czechoslovakia even before the communist takeover, would have anticipated seeing a liberal intellectual, Vaclav Havel, installed as President with a specifically Christian ritual of dedication in Prague's Wenceslas Cathedral? This episode reminds us how deep is the need for a transcendent reference at important junctures in the life of nations and communities, as well as of individuals. It also suggests that a religious frame strengthens shared values. The power of implicit Christian meaning in our apparently secular world should not be underestimated, even when the explicit manifestations of faith seem feeble.

There are, of course, vital differences between the situation of the churches in Britain and in Eastern Europe. The low ebb of religious activity in Britain cannot be attributed to the aggressive atheism of a repressive state controlled by a foreign power. The new flowering of Christianity in Eastern Europe is undoubtedly at least in part a consequence of the way in which the repression of religion turned the churches into a natural channel for alternative values and made them a symbolic focus of nationalist feelings. Britain – or more accurately England – has suffered neither religious persecution from outside nor any sustained threat to her national identity for a very long time. The absence of such threats may in part explain why the community can afford to keep religion quietly on the back burner or, changing

101

the metaphor, to use the church as a kind of pilot light, ready to burst into flame should Christianity or nationhood ever come under open threat. These are sociological, not theological, considerations. They simply suggest how it is possible to regard the characteristic tendency of the British people to be the sleeping partner in a compact with the church as in some sense 'natural' – that is, naturalistically explicable.

We need, however, to press the argument to the point where the sociological and the theological intersect, in order to make clear the general theoretical position which underlies the discussion in this book. The metaphor of faith as a flame suggests that it is a mistake to expect belief to take forest fire proportions – dramatic, fierce and all-consuming – for most people most of the time. Human life largely consists of the mundane and the humdrum; human identity must be specific and local before it can encompass any wider sympathy. Of all bodies, a Christian church, committed to a doctrine of incarnation, must take seriously the local habitations through which our humanity is shaped and mediated. They cannot be transcended or transfigured unless they are first grounded, earthed and accepted. The church, therefore, works with and through specific experiences of ordinary human life. Indeed, it is one of the most distinctive and potent features of Christianity that it conceives the mundane as the proper vehicle for the transcendent. Everyday life is, therefore, an appropriate base from which to glimpse the transcendent possibility and not merely a low level secular foil against which to measure virtuoso and heroic spiritual feats. No one, therefore, has to be apologetic about the unheroic and unspectacular nature of much that the church habitually does.

The Need for Meaning

Further, however, a specifically Christian dimension, wholly separate from and uncontaminated by the ordinary stuff of social relationships and institutional life, does not have to be conceived. Human life is at the same moment both fallen – broken and fractured – and the medium of redemptive possibility. This persistent duality provides the church with its dilemmas and with its opportunities. When clergy, for example, are asked to lend the resources of the church and the authority of the sacred to the celebration of some aspect of 'tribalism' – civic life, family rites of passage, the activities of the workplace, state ceremonial – they are often uncomfortable and become acutely aware of the fallen nature of human life and its institutions. They itch for a prophetic role, through exercise of which they can confidently pass judgement on this fallenness. Yet a church which disdains involvement in natural human tribalism – people's celebration of who and what they are – is unlikely to get much of a hearing when it actually confronts the fallen and the flawed aspects of our individual lives and the wider world.

In the broadest anthropological terms, the need for meaning is the fundamental human requirement. This does not have to be religious meaning or even a consistent and coherent scheme of meaning. Most of the time individuals simply experience meaning as inhering in those habitual patterns of life which are taken for granted. It is pragmatic, fragmented, a rag-bag of symbol and habit. Individuals and maybe whole societies can get by without resort to religious meaning, although there does seem to be a powerful and recurrent desire for a transcendent reference.

What is essential, however, is to have some means by which the power of the irrational and non-rational features of life can be acknowledged and brought into the sphere of meaning. In this respect ritual and habit are often more crucial than formal beliefs. What the church does in its liturgies and ceremonials and simply through its institutional existence – just being there – is important and effective for people beyond, and sometimes in spite of the extent to which they rationally accept or reject the theological propositions which underlie these acts.

For the present argument, what matters is the role of the Church of England in the business of creating and affirming meaning in British society. Historically the Christian faith, and for the last four hundred years that faith particularly as embodied in the national church, has provided the clearest, most systematic-ally articulated and authoritative source of overarching meaning. What makes it incredibly difficult to assess precisely how secular British society may have become (or how secular it may have been in, say, the eighteenth century) is the fact that the church has for many centuries acted as the specialist institution which

103

guards and expresses the ground of Christian meaning *on behalf of* the rest of the population. The passivity of the nominally Christian laity and the amorphous and indistinct content of folk religiosity need to be set in this context. The invisibility of common religion is counterbalanced by the visibility of the church and its official functionaries. Earlier chapters have included examples of how individuals, communities, government and nation seem still to turn to the church when crisis fractures the pragmatic assumption of taken-for-granted meaning. The church at that moment is expected to have the answer, to repair the fracture and to move meaning to a higher plane.

At the same time the church has also been woven into the symbolic structures of identity and belonging which are expressed through the celebratory aspects of meaning. Neither of these roles – the vicarious guardianship of Christian meaning and the affirmation of identity – is without its dangers. The first allows the Christian commitment of the mass of people to be whittled away through disuse; and the second can result in a flaccid acceptance of things as they happen to be. The hazard may be noticed, even if it cannot be escaped. For both of these roles and their attendant dangers are part of the church's necessary implication in the mundane.

The Influence of History

But a caveat is now needed. It is possible that the church is steadily losing its role as holder, and when required articulator, of overarching meaning. A powerful case can be made, for example, for considering the new mass media as serious rivals in the business of offering meaning in modern (or, as some would say, secular, fragmented, image-saturated post-modern) society. The question, however, remains open. The readiness with which people still reach for the church, and especially for its senior functionaries – vicars, bishops and the archbishop – to plug gaps in meaning and celebrate identity suggests that at least an important residue of the role remains in place.

Many of the roles which, it is argued in this book, the church should accept, arise in paradoxical ways out of historical features which cause problems and even offence to some bodies of

Christian opinion. Among these establishment is prominent. Yet in an important sense constitutional disestablishment would make little difference at the levels with which we are concerned. Establishment has involved notorious difficulties in the relations of church and state. But there is little doubt that it is the fact of having been the state church for so long which has woven the Church of England so minutely into the fabric of identity of society and nation and has given its leaders that sometimes unwelcome task of being representatives and mediators. The parish system derives its strengths and contradictions from its place in the Tudor settlement, which made it a problematic but fruitful semi-anachronism from the outset. The Church of England was created as an institution of universal national belonging, with the rights and duties which that position entails, in a context of limited religious toleration and ultimately of openly religious plurality. This fact underlies many of the problems and potentialities of unclear boundary definition – Who is the church? Are there any limits to the pastoral responsibilities of the clergy? What roles has the episcopate? Where are the 'centre' and the 'periphery' of the church?

This lack of clarity is also compounded and enriched by a further historical feature of the Church of England. From the time of its nationalization under the Tudors the church managed to incorporate change within a recognizable – in that sense a 'traditional' – frame, and has found ways of encompassing a variety of theological emphases and styles of churchmanship under one hospitable umbrella. Modern tendencies to centralization in more than one centre and to bureaucratization may put new strains on this ancient flexibility. The fragmentation evident in the abandonment of common prayer may be symptomatic of a more general weakening of this principle of universalism. Perhaps it is even a splintering which reflects 'post-modern' conditions and at some level mirrors the secular world in which life-styles proliferate and a restless pursuit of the new energizes consumption.

The Principle of Universalism

A major social change which might be expected to pose a challenge to the church's tradition of universalism is the existence of ethnic minorities who enthusiastically practise non-Christian religions. This throws into sharp relief the semi-secularized passivity of the British mainstream. It also exposes the fragility of a religious toleration which is very often based on the assumption that religion in Britain is neither precise nor demanding for any except its official functionaries. Yet even in this multi-faith setting the clergy and bishops are frequently looked to as natural leaders and conciliators in those conflicts which affect religious and ethnic minorities, even by the leaders of those groups themselves. The legal principle of universal belonging to the Church of England is an anachronism. But the privileged position of the clergy of the Church of England, which derives from that principle, is a continuing reality which poses problems and opens unlikely – and hitherto undiscerned – doors for them. It is worth examining this position of privilege and leadership more closely.

The role of the Church of England within the British religious pattern constitutes a unique case. It is neither the flourishing voluntarism of the USA – open religious competition in a free market – nor the unchallenged Protestantism of the Scandinavian Lutheran established churches, which produces a level of religious practice even lower than that of England. It is further still from the Latin pattern, in which old Catholic monopolies face militant anticlerical secularism. The British configuration is a modified semi-monopoly. An established national church spanning Protestant and Catholic tendencies coexists, today for the most part in ecumenical amity, with rival churches and denominations. To these have been added in the last forty years the religions of the ethnic minorities drawn largely from the New Commonwealth.

Historically the British churches ran roughly parallel to the strata of the emerging modern class structure, although that association has today lost some of its erstwhile clarity. At all events, it is generally accepted that the Church of England was traditionally associated with the gentry stratum which occupied the apex of the social system. This aristocratic church played an important role in an extraordinary process during the nineteenth century: the new industrial bourgeoisie and the old landed class engaged in an exchange by which new money was gentrified and a radical reform of manners and morals was effected, largely through the Evangelical revival. What emerged was not only a non-revolutionary and only moderately antagonistic pattern of class relationships but a new prominence for the reformed Church of England in the symbolism of national and communal self-consciousness. Church and monarchy alike emerged as icons of national identity out of a situation in which, before Victoria, both had been dangerously corrupt and likely to fall. Today we see the legacy of that process with some paradoxical new twists.

In the first place, the church has lost much of its direct power. Many things have contributed to this, including the democratization of political culture and changes in the social recruitment of the clergy. One curious, but important, corollary of this is that as the church has lost power it has in some ways correspondingly gained authority. The church's gentry connotations have lost many of the negative features which they had when incumbents enjoyed the substance of arbitrary power in the community and bishops wielded political clout in Parliament. Relatively few clergy today are, objectively speaking, products of the gentry culture. Yet a benevolent image of the church as redolent of a more gentlemanly world is a staple cliché of popular culture. It is a long while since the Church of England was straightforwardly the Tory Party at prayer. The observable inaccuracy of this popular image, however, suggests that something interesting is going on here. The church, it seems, sits beneath a canopy of inherited position and authority – social and political status as well as the weight of the sacred itself – without enjoying real secular power. Yet status without power allows the church to be generally respected and rarely disliked. Its very loss of power makes it possible for people to see it as above party politics and thus a natural, if idealized, mediator and conciliator, representing something – whether community or nation – *as a whole*.

A Church above Politics

This role of standing beyond and above the politics of special interests gives the Church of England a continuing potential influence on the life of the nation. Unfortunately it also entails a version of Catch 22. For it ensures that cries of rage and distress will be voiced whenever the church's representatives stray, whether deliberately or inadvertently, into the arena of party politics. The outrage will come from both ends and the middle of the political spectrum alike. The church, especially its leaders, and Prince Charles share both a status and a problem: their dilemma is how to engage with the serious issues of the day without jeopardizing that very non-political status from which flows the authority to speak on behalf of the whole people.

There is a further difficulty. The attribution to the church of an authority beyond mere politics can lead both clergy and laity into a well-intentioned hubris. The church is increasingly expected – and sometimes expects itself – to solve the most fundamental and intractable problems which have confounded the political parties, from global warming to the decline of the old industrial areas and the problems of the inner cities. In addition, of course, it is routinely expected to solve all those problems which are intrinsically not amenable to political and economic solutions – bereavement, war, grief, loss, ageing, mortality and the rest.

> The minister, as he goes about his job as a representative of the church on the boundary with the rest of society, has a great deal of hope invested in him. He is asked to show dependability and reassurance, while recognising at times that within the church and within himself there is much uncertainty and confusion . . . To some extent they [the ministers] are asked to solve the insoluble, cure the incurable, and make reality go away . . . For the church the dependent posture is itself a reality that cannot be made to go away – without it the church as an institution could scarcely exist – so it is something constantly to be worked with.[1]

The agenda is unrealistic, but it is easy to see how the historic role of the Church of England has contributed to such expectations. In the circumstances the church often makes a creditable stab at the impossible.

One final feature of the church's privileged position and its popular, if partly inaccurate association of gentry status, calls for comment. Anachronistic images of the church as Barchester may look quaint, sentimental, embarrassing and false. But they express something important which the earlier consideration of the role of cathedrals addressed. These institutions have become short-hand for most of the things which are conspicuously lacking in the contemporary world. They deny the inevitability of change, insecurity, stress, anonymity and the dominance of the inanimate machine. Thus the cathedral as a centre for tourism (or pilgrimage) focuses this profound desire to exorcise modernity for a space. Consider the Cathedral Close – closed to the car, turned into a civil and civilized pedestrian precinct – through which our old cathedrals are approached. For many visitors it surely stands for a vanished way of life in which the pace was slower, identity was secure, and life was less full of problems. Life was, of course, never like that; nostalgia is selective and mendacious. But the church cannot escape the difficult and mostly unwelcome role of somehow standing for pre-modern certainties. Its functionaries cannot choose the demands which people place on the church, only respond as best they may within the frame which history has created for both church and people.

Note

1. W. G. Lawrence and E. J. Miller, quoted in Wesley Carr, *The Priestlike Task* (London, SPCK, 1985), p. 18.

10
THEOLOGY FOR THE CHURCH'S FUTURE

To write a theology of church and ministry in so brief a space as this is impossible. However, the practical argument of this book cannot stand alone. All Christian thinking has to be marked by critical reflection on the concepts about God, church and world which undergird and inspire action. The themes suggested in this chapter are themselves traditionally Anglican – the doctrine of the incarnation and a church based in trinitarian theology. At the end, however, it is suggested that it is in the crucial area of linking thinking about God with the realities of the work of the church that thinking in the Church of England has recently been deficient. As intermediate themes, therefore, the notes or marks of the church are reaffirmed. The basic ideas in this chapter were produced by Wesley Carr.

It would be presumptuous to think that in so short a chapter a full theology could be provided for the church's future. Yet something has to be attempted. The Church of England, as we have noted, lays claim to a distinctive ministry within the spectrum of the life of the Church of God. Its history has been marked by an attractive pragmatism. Yet of itself this is not enough for any church. All its activity needs to stand perpetually under the critical judgement of a theological interpretation of its understanding of itself and its ministry. This is especially true today, when so-called 'historic' justifications alone no longer function without question, and when ecumenical advances push each church to a more self-examining stance than it may hitherto have had to adopt. If, therefore, we are to seek to justify any claim that the Church of

England both has and should have a future, we need to do more than demonstrate the distinctive way in which it has functioned both in history and the present, with individuals, groups and society; we have also to affirm theological grounds for this justification. In this chapter we shall maintain that such a theology is incarnational in style, trinitarian in structure and confident in its critical pragmatism.

The Incarnational Style

The Anglican style of theological thinking has been characterized as incarnational. The Church of England's historical development through the Reformation and since, and its intimacy with national and cultural life, have naturally and inevitably produced thinking on the incarnation. In particular its life from the nineteenth century to the present has been marked by attention to the doctrine, in the work of such figures as Gore, Temple, Ramsey and, more recently and with rather different stances, Wiles, Houlden and Sykes. In addition it is noteworthy that when working clergy are asked to reflect on their activity and understanding of ministry, they seem instinctively to employ language of 'presence'. This applies as much to parochial clergy as to those engaged in sector ministry, such as chaplains in prisons, schools or industry. If, however, we are to choose an incarnational basis as theological justification for ministry, we need a doctrine which is itself inherently strong and not merely an expression of feeling. Otherwise what passes for Christian behaviour based upon the model of incarnation becomes a disguised claim to a privilege, which could properly be forfeit at any time. From time to time so-called theological interpretations of a distinctively Anglican ministry slip into this error.

The contemporary problems inherent in the doctrine of the incarnation have been frequently rehearsed. When incarnation is regarded as a sort of enshrining rather than a model of engagement the doctrine degenerates. Yet popular incarnational thinking drifts towards enshrining. Jesus becomes a chocolate Father Christmas: he looks like a human being on the outside but inside is all soft and divine. This incidentally conforms to some people's view of vicars. From outside they look like any other

111

human being, but inside they are somehow different. When, then, they display human frailty, they are regarded as somehow failing to be what they should be. They begin to represent the enshrining of God, with its attendant dangers. The enshrining idea of the incarnation cannot be abandoned. It possesses, for example, the power to inspire Christian worship. But the associated problem is that it may also convey notions of superiority and privilege. What is enshrined is believed to be superior and the shrine becomes a place of privilege where power is exercised. Casual use of the doctrine of the incarnation can thus become inimical to ministry.

The theme of the incarnation, however, is not one of shrines and privilege. Indeed some modern theological work on incarnation is probably a reaction against such a tendency. It emphasizes that when we speak about God incarnate we are talking dynamically of engagement and of risk. This point becomes clearer when we consider the basic structure of the doctrine. Whenever the person of Jesus Christ is considered, we are confronted with two-ness. John Robinson, a bishop with a knack for the phrase that summarizes, said somewhere that the problem of the incarnation is essentially that of trying to put two billiard balls on the same spot. There is an intrinsic and inescapable two-ness: Father/Son; Jesus of Nazareth/Christ of Faith; God/man; Flesh/Spirit.

The effect is that no view of God, Christ or mankind can be held without sustaining a tension. But we need to be clear. This is not a reaffirmation of the pattern of thesis–antithesis–synthesis. That style seeks to reconcile and resolve tensions. Nor is this a theology of paradox, however noble it seems to hold tensions unresolved for their own sake. Both of these positions are undermined by Christian experience, not least that of worship. The contemporary thrust towards dynamic thinking on the incarnation suggests the following definition: the doctrine of the incarnation is about temporary or fragmentary resolutions of tension which produce a basis for effective action.

There are obvious connections between this proposition and the concepts of ministry that have been discussed earlier. An interpretative ministry has to seize its moments and opportunities as they occur. This indeed is the mark of the ministry of Jesus himself. The word – whether it be parable, word of comfort, or profound interpretation of life – is itself momentary and inevitably incomplete. But because something is ephemeral it is not necessarily unimportant. Every experienced minister is familiar with the complexity of the overall process: the doctrine of the incarnation points us to the importance of what is momentary.

The glory of God and human dignity, for instance, cannot be permanently aligned: that would be heaven or the final realization of the Kingdom of God. But when people adopt, or (perhaps better) are claimed by, the paradigm of God's investment in mankind, then fragmentarily or momentarily that human glory and divine manifestation coincide. It is in that hope, as St Paul says, that we are saved (Romans 8.24). Incarnationally based faith, thought and action will, therefore, consistently focus not on identification, with its implicitly static ideas, but on the dynamics implied by differentiation. This perception needs more exploration than is possible here. But it prevents us succumbing to any temptation to become casual. Differentiation is an essential component if interpretative engagement with others – ministry – is to be possible.[1]

There is, however, one further contextual point to hold in mind. There is today a growing mistrust of dualism in any form. Religiously, for instance, the New Age phenomenon is based upon a dogmatic anti-dualist stance. In this context the Christian doctrine of the incarnation will be all the more under question, since two-ness is unavoidable. But when we grasp that incarnation is about engagement rather than presence, then we have an approach which can be constructively employed.

To address this issue we need the rigour and clarification provided by serious reflection on the theme of incarnation. We should not confuse identification and differentiation. Identification is too simplistic. In Jesus Christ God did not become 'one of us'. The two-nesses in the incarnation are designed to ensure that we avoid such a divinizing trap. We cannot speak of identification without a 'because clause': 'God became man "because . . ." or "so that . . .".' The divine intention must always be discerned and articulated.

If we recognize that communication is a dimension of ministry, when seen as interpretation, we might say that God became human so that he might communicate more effectively with his human creation. But for communication to take place, a twofold stance is essential. The communicator needs as much a sense of self-identity as recognition of the other. The idea of incarnation is not simply about identification with people. It stands for engagement with purpose or, as we have previously suggested, ministry as interpretation.

Interpretation as Systematic Local Theology

To be able to interpret does not call for specialist knowledge, although some is required, since it is expected. Nor is interpretation the same as understanding: these are two different activities. Interpretation is about gaining a perspective and risking it. As a theme it exposes a neglected dimension to ministry. Because churches and clergy may have been preoccupied with retaining a presence and so making a disguised claim to the authority of the church – 'being there' – the function of the vicar as local theologian, the interpreter who works, as it were, on the hoof, has been diminished. Clergy then tend to fulfil their own caricatures as those who care and do good, and the more competent train in therapeutic skills and approaches. The vicar, however, on the basis of an incarnational stance is not identified by trying to become one with those around or differentiated in the sense of being set apart. Rather he or she is a local theologian, engaged not so much in telling but interpreting.

This task requires skill. But it is also the enacting of systematic theology. For it means bringing together in public the human experience with which the vicar makes some identification and the theological tradition by which he or she is differentiated. Working ministers sometimes ask, 'How do we do theology?' The thrust of the question is towards applied or practical theology. But more important is the question, 'Why now attempt the enterprise at all?' Clergy like others today are busy people, with less time for reflection than they would wish. It is no use urging an impossible standard of aloofness from these dynamics of everyday life. Opportunities for theological reflection seem to be declining in the present day world. Yet to think theologically is the essence of the practice of ministry, since in so doing we attempt to connect two constants: (1) envisioning God, or what is usually called the tradition; and (2) the issues which are stimulated in us by experience, the contemporary situation.

> The theocentric character of any genuinely theological statement, whether explicitly or implicitly addressed, drives every theologian to claims to truth which demand publicness and, at the limit, universality . . . Theologians, therefore, in collaborative, interdisciplinary work with their colleagues, need to ask what after all is the present meaning and truth of the interpreted tradition and the interpreted contemporary situation, by focusing on those fundamental questions constituting particular religious questions and those fundamental responses constituting particular religious traditions, and on establishing mutually critical correlations between both sets of interpretation.[2]

The theological undergirding of the structure (the parochial system) and the stance of ministry (interpretation – as we have outlined it in the above chapters) lies in the systematic work on the doctrine of the incarnation.

The Trinitarian Structure

A recent survey of the theological assumptions which underlay the curriculum for training ministers in colleges and courses showed that almost all employed a trinitarian argument.[3] If the style of the ministry of the Church of England is incarnational in style, it is trinitarian in structure. Under this heading of the Trinity a series of theological themes are held together. Among these are ideas of relationship between people, whether as individuals or in groups – a core issue of ministry. But alongside is essentially held the parallel concept of relatedness. By this is meant the way in which in a human organization, such as a family, an industry or a church, interaction between people is not confined to the direct contacts of relationship. The shared sense of an institution affects people's behaviour. The managing director, for instance, may never actually have a relationship with the floor-sweeper in a large industry, but their behaviour and that of others is affected by the connection that they have, their relatedness – both having a role within the total enterprise. Some awareness of this dimension to institutional life is essential for church leaders, such as bishops. Always pressed for more intimate relationship, they need to have a grasp of the continuing relatedness that makes up the life of the church.

There is, however, more to the trinitarian model. It not only illuminates the internal interactions that mark the life of the church; it also, and more importantly for ministry, emphasizes the connection between internal coherence and missionary activity and points to that imaginative creativity which is the mark of God's presence. And the idea of unity that it fosters is not static. The traditional description of the activity of the Trinity – *opera* (NB 'activity') *trinitatis ad extra indivisa sunt* (the external activity of the Trinity presents itself as undivided) – describes a dynamic, creative unity, such as we might also expect to be the mark of the church.

This is not the place for a long excursus on the Trinity, even though exploration of that theme will be increasingly needed as the church seeks a more profound and satisfying theological model for its ministry and, particularly in the Decade of Evangelism, its mission. The key question, both organizationally and theologically, is 'Where is this grounded?'

It is a characteristic of Christian doctrine that the most wide-ranging and most speculative ideas have to be rooted in the most accessible, and sometimes what seem to be trivial, dimensions of life and doctrine. Christian convictions about God, for instance, must incorporate reflections on the incarnation. That in turn is inseparable from issues of humanity, and not just humanity in an idealized form but in its most 'real' – suffering and death. The point was classically grasped and expressed early in the history of the Church in the probably pre-Pauline hymn in Philippians 2.5ff. Small things axiomatically possess intrinsic importance.

The Usefulness of the Marks of the Church

To make this connection we need to recover some intermediate, or (we might call them) transitional ideas. The study of the implicit assumptions made by colleges and courses noted that the most common structure of argument was from the idea of God (usually described in some trinitarian fashion) to that of ministry and thence to some concept of the church. This is not a particular failure by theological teachers; they and their colleges are in this area aligned with the contemporary church. The Church of England has become so preoccupied with ministries, diaconal, presbyteral and episcopal, that it has failed to give sufficient attention to its distinctive ecclesiology.

Obviously in one sense we might argue that all discussions on ministry are implicitly eccesiological. But that will not do. Without attention to an earthed ecclesiology – that is, an interpretation of the nature and activity of the church – debate on ministries will become increasingly incestuous and irrelevant to the life of the church. It may be that the current feeling of sterility, which ministers sometimes express, is not so much the result of secularizing influences and the withdrawal of people from the proffered ministry of the church as a tendency towards an 'in-house' assumption about the nature of the ministry, which pervades discussion.

A recent example of this trend can be found in *Episcopal Ministry: The Report of the Archbishops' Group on The Episcopate, 1990*. The book includes many useful and interesting data. But the authors consistently become stuck at two points: first, the specific nature of the Church of England as a church; and second, the limitations of conducting any discussion about one particular ministry in isolation from the others. That is not to say that the working party did not perceive these two issues. But whenever they arise, they seem to have to be set on one side.

One useful set of intermediate or transitional concepts which both earth the trinitarian structure of the church's ministry and hold the doctrine of the church in place, as it were, between the Trinity and that ministry has been articulated as the 'marks' or 'notes' of the church. These were initially three, taken from the Nicene Creed: 'I believe in one holy, catholic and apostolic church', and so might be given some significance within the Church of England, which acknowledges this creed. Subsequently, however, the idea was chiefly employed in the pre-reformation Church as a justification of papal power and after the Reformation seems to have been of most interest to Catholic thinkers. The theme was also used in the nineteenth century by Tractarian

117

writers as a demonstration of the catholicity of the Church of England. In particular they emphasized four marks: unity, holiness, catholicity and apostolicity.

This history seems to imply that the marks are the possession of only one wing of the Church of England. Probably most Evangelicals, for example, are not familiar with them. We cannot, therefore, lightly assume that they are self-evidently useful as the intermediate concepts which are needed between Trinity and ministry. Nevertheless they might come into renewed and less partisan prominence partly because of current ecumenical discussion about the church and partly because they are originally not specifically theses of Roman Catholic ecclesiology but credally based concepts.

Carefully considered, these notes bring into association aspects of God and marks of earthed church life. The first is unity. In the Trinity the unity of the Godhead is discerned as not static but continually being discovered in relationship. In a simple sense, we may claim that the more activity there is between the persons, the more united is the external expression. In other words, through *opera* (the work of God) the mission of God and his internal coherence are both furthered.

The second, apostolicity, draws our attention further to the essential outgoingness of God in his perpetual mission. Seen in this light, the task of the church in evangelism and pastoral activity is hardly discussable. It constitutes an essence of the church, without which there is no church. It may be especially useful in the Decade of Evangelism for the Church of England to contribute this insight, which is intrinsic to its practical pastoring and to its distinctive ecclesiology.

The third mark, holiness, is, when used of God, his divinity as expressed through creativity. This includes the capacity to imagine and so bring into being new worlds. Because of this dimension to God, he is inevitably awesome and awful. Here we are drawn into worship, not just as respect but as participation in such imaginative creativity. Again, the Church of England has hitherto prided itself on its concern in liturgy to sustain the necessary distance from God, however intimate the invited relationship, if human beings are to live with God and share in his purposes. If they are to do this, they need to share his holiness – itself an awesome thought.

Finally we have the note of catholicity, which while appearing to be more concerned with the church than with God, is not necessarily so. We can conceive the nature of God in his dealings with his creation as marked by sustained coherence imbued with mystery, which might be a wide definition of catholicity. The world dimension to notions of 'catholic' and 'ecumenical' has been one of the great rediscoveries of our era. When it is in danger of being lost to a defensive pietism, it can be revived not by exhortation to a wider awareness but by recognition of this mark of the Christian church. It is regrettable that some of those in the Church of England who claim the word 'catholic' have been those who have given a lead in the flight from this concept.

The Connection with the Church of England

The interpretative ministry and the parochial system of the Church of England illuminate these marks and are undergirded by them. Unity, for instance, in a parochial church can never be a private preoccupation of the congregation. The concept is always expanded to one of genuine *oecoumene* – the whole inhabited world in a specific locality. Holiness is the transformation of all human life (again a parochial idea) through its being represented before God by the worship and life of the members of a Christian congregation. The theme of apostolicity always directs thoughts away from their source, in this case away from the necessary self-awareness of the congregation, towards the larger world rather than to their own small concerns. Catholicity draws our attention to the universality of such a task, transcending the boundaries of the parish, however necessary these are for practical purposes.

To recover attention to these marks of the church will provide a way by which the felt realities of church life in the Church of England – crucially its parochial opportunities and interpretative ministry – are linked to the structural theology of the Trinity and so continually brought under scrutiny. There is much more to be done here. More important, however, for our present purposes is the way in which the theme of the Trinity, earthed through the marks of the church, links the reality of power and the need for authority.

Throughout the previous chapters this has been a persistent theme. Power and authority stand in uneasy relation in today's

119

Church of England. There is a widespread assumption that some exercise of power – whether by bishops, clergy, laity, synod, or even God – could rescue the Church of England from its dilemmas and either restore it to its former glory or bring it into a new form of existence. For example, important questions about the way in which a church might structure authority are reduced to issues of hierarchy of power. The argument concerns relations between bishops and clergy or, even more prominently at present, clergy and laity. These are compounded by the new forum which is provided for public rumination on the problem and private internecine struggles for power. What is avoided (although even this is speciously present in the many discussions of ministry) is the theme of order and orders. The two are connected, not just in historical and quasi-theological discussion of ordination, but in the day-to-day issues of authority in the church.

Critical Pragmatism

We have noted that the issues facing the Church of England are not peculiar to the church: they are endemic in contemporary Western societies. It is unlikely, therefore, that the church will easily settle for itself something that the rest of the world cannot resolve. It is also improbable that a book like this will reach a confident conclusion on the topic. Nevertheless, in the face of the irrational expectations, of which the church (especially the Church of England) is a focus, more is needed than sociological understanding of what is happening or organizational clarity of role, important though both are. Some way is required of enabling the church as a body to remain strong enough internally to face the destructive delusions (always vigorous in religion) of power. It is also needed so that the world, which for a variety of overt and covert reasons looks to the church, will find in it a form of transformed realism, which is the mark of an institution which is immersed in this world but with transcendent awareness. Or, as described earlier, a church whose *raison d'être* is marked by an incarnational style, a trinitarian structure and a critical pragmatism.

The traditional means to this end has been through the connection between order in the church and orders of ministry.

Order offers sufficient coherence for people to know to what they belong. The danger is obviously that such order may drift towards repressive forms of control. But so that there can be beneficial order, differentiation of people through the creation of orders becomes necessary. It is interesting to note that no church seems to have been able to sustain interactive behaviour with its context, whether in social care, pastoral ministry or evangelistic fervour, without rapidly arranging itself through orders. The reason for this is not solely that human groups tend to conform to familiar patterns of organization. Nor is it purely a matter of the people's dependent need for the reassurance of hierarchy. Both have their place. But in the case of the church the concept of orders also derives from the relationship and relatedness of the being of God in Trinity. Without differentiation there, the vision of God becomes static. Such a God may be feared, possibly even admired. But he will not be loved and so struggled with.

The same is true of the church. A body which under the guise of egalitarianism, reinforced by a blinkered reading of Scripture, attempts to obliterate all working differences of role is likely to become self-sufficient. It may then be admired for its supposed consistency but probably ignored in regard to any serious matters. It is not sufficiently differentiated and frayed enough at the edges for people to make contact with it. The church which we have described needs to be tattered at its edges: that is the mark of its incarnational style. But to sustain such a stance, it also needs the differentiation of orders, not least so as constantly to remind its members that the world is not as simple as they might think and, even more importantly, that the trinitarian God is not as casually accessible as they might wish to believe.

When, therefore, there is a persistent discussion of whether the church should have (other than for antiquarian reasons) clergy who are differentiated from the laity – and, of course, *vice versa* – the debate is not without profound implications for the theology of the church. The ministry which we have discerned and for which we believe there is a future certainly implies the continuance of differentiated ministries. Chief among these is the order of 'vicar'. While this is not one of the traditional definitions of an order, it might be that established in the incarnation and

121

earthed in the Trinity, this is one important consequence of that critical pragmatism which has marked, and will have to mark, the continuance of the Church of England.

Notes

1. See further Wesley Carr, *The Pastor as Theologian* (London, SPCK, 1990).
2. David Tracy, *The Analogical Imagination* (London, SCM Press, 1981), pp. 80–1.
3. First published as *Ordination and the Church's Ministry: A Theological Evaluation* (London, ACCM, 1990).

INDEX

125

Index

Jenkins, David 68

laity, differentiated from clergy
121

media ch. 7 *passim*
meaning, need for 102–4
ministry: interpretative 16–17,
119; working theology for 26–8,
ch. 10 *passim*; 'every member'
43; selection for 47–50;
trinitarian basis 115–16
Muslim leaders 61

non-stipendiary ministry 23–4

orders 121–2

Parochial Church Council 89
parochial system: in principle 17;
expectations within ch. 2
passim; and communities 45–6;
gossip within 73–5; 'national
parish' 82
politics and the church 107–9
Portsmouth Cathedral 65
prophecy 69

Ramsey, Michael 12
religion 39
representation ch. 4 *passim*;
different forms 96–8
Riches, Kenneth 68

Robinson, John 112
Runcie, Robert 12, 58, 60
Rushdie, Salman 61

Santer, Mark 85
Sheppard, Dick 67–8
Swaggart, Jimmy 79
Synod, Deanery 57
Synod, Diocesan 91
Synod, General: increasing
prominence 56–7; and bishops
ch. 8 *passim*
synodical system: and episcopacy
10, 44, 88–91

televangelism 79
television 76–81
Thatcher, Margaret 58
Thompson, Jim 21
Tiller, John 24
Toynbee, Philip 64–5
Tracy, David 122n
transcendence 69–71, 102
trinitarian theology 115–16

Vanstone, William 61
vicar: demand for 35;
representative ch. 4 *passim*
vocation 47

Whale, John 79
Woodforde, Parson, of Weston
Longueville 54–5